THE OPEN UNIVERSITY

An Arts Foundation Course
Units 1-2A

An Introduction to the Study of the Humanities

Prepared for the Course Team by Arthur Marwick, Ellie Mace, John Ferguson, and Arnold Kettle

The Open University Press

The Open University Press
Walton Hall Milton Keynes

First published 1981 (but incorporating material previously published in A101 Units 1–2A (1978) and A100 Unit 4 (1970)). Reprinted 1981.

Designed by the Graphic Design Group of the Open University.

Printed in Great Britain by
EYRE AND SPOTTISWOODE LIMITED
AT GROSVENOR PRESS PORTSMOUTH

ISBN 0 335 05410 2

This text forms part of an Open University course. The complete list of units in the course appears at the end of this text.

For general availability of supporting material referred to in this text please write to Open University Educational Enterprises Limited, 12 Cofferidge Close, Stony Stratford, Milton Keynes MK11 1BY, Great Britain.

Further information on Open University courses may be obtained from the Admissions Office, The Open University, P.O. Box 48, Walton Hall, Milton Keynes, MK7 6AB.

1.2

CONTENTS

IMPORTANT NOTE

You will see that this correspondence text is numbered 'Units 1–2A'. This means that you should be working on it during the first week and *the first part of the second week* of your study of the course. The next correspondence text you will receive, *Uses and Abuses of Argument*, is numbered 'Units 2B and 9' and you should work on the appropriate sections of it during *the second part of the second week* and during the ninth week of the course. For a fuller explanation of the way your study time should be divided, consult the Course Guide.

As you work through the correspondence text, you will need to consult your Colour Supplement and the course reader, *Nature and Industrialization*.

INTRODUCTION: THE FOUR AIMS OF THE COURSE
(by Arthur Marwick)

Universities, in a rough and ready, but commonsense sort of way, tend to get divided up into faculties of science, technology, social science, and arts (and most universities have faculties of medicine and faculties of law as well). I do not imagine there are any difficulties over these distinctions: science contains physics and chemistry and molecular biology and so on; social science contains sociology, geography, politics and government, and so on; the arts contain history, philosophy, literature, and so on. (Some institutions, and most schools, say 'English' rather than 'literature'; but we do not teach languages in our faculty of arts, so literature covers both English literature and, on occasion, the literature – in translation – of other countries as well). In some universities these days, people say 'faculty of humanities' rather than 'faculty of arts'. What these people have in mind is that 'the arts' should perhaps mean actually *practising* the arts, that is to say actually painting, composing or performing music, or writing novels or poetry; talking of 'the humanities' stresses that the concern is with *studying* these arts rather than actually creating them, and also makes it easier to bring in such subjects as history and philosophy. For myself, I prefer the phrase 'the humanities'. However, the agreed title for this course that you are now embarking on is 'An Arts Foundation Course' and the title of this introduction might as well, for all practical purposes, be 'An Introduction to the Study of the Arts'.

In our Arts Faculty the subjects (but 'subjects' is a rather vague word, so instead we tend to use a more precise, but unfortunately rather pompous one, 'disciplines') we cover are history, literature, music, philosophy, and art history; we also teach the study of religion, and some of that comes into this foundation course, classical studies and the history of science, both of which do not come into the foundation course. So, when in this course we use phrases like 'the arts disciplines', or 'the disciplines you have studied', or 'the humanities', we mean history, literature, music, philosophy, history of art, and religious studies (though, as you will find later, there is some debate as to whether religious studies should be seen as a discipline in itself, or whether it is rather a mixture of disciplines).

Now perhaps you are a little intimidated by the wide range of subjects (or 'disciplines' as I shall have to call them from now on) covered in this foundation course. Perhaps you feel your prime interest to be in history and have something of a suspicion of poetry or painting. Perhaps, on the other hand, you are a practising musician yourself or regularly visit the art galleries. Perhaps, at the moment, you have no very clear idea of what your interest is. Thus, the first thing for all of us is to try to be absolutely clear what exactly this foundation course is about. That is why we have spelled out the four aims of the course. In this introduction I am simply going to explain more fully each of the aims in turn; and in this task I am assisted by John Ferguson, who (before he left the Open University) was the first Course Team Chairman of the Arts Foundation Course, Arnold Kettle, who is Professor of Literature, and Ellie Mace, who is the Institute of Educational Technology member attached to the Course Team.

Now, carefully read through these four aims of the course:

Aim 1

To stimulate your interest in and enthusiasm for the study of the arts, and to provide a foundation for further more detailed study at post-foundation level.

Aim 2

To help you develop the basic skills of clear and logical thinking, and of selecting relevant material, interpreting it, and expressing yourself in good English prose, and to introduce you to what is meant by education and the learning process at university level.

Aim 3

To introduce you to the separate purposes and methods of the different individual disciplines in the arts.

Aim 4

But nevertheless to stress the general idea that the Arts disciplines should not be kept in separate compartments but can and should be brought together both in the study of particular problems and in any comprehensive study of the values and standards of civil society.

1 THE FIRST AIM OF THE COURSE
(by Arthur Marwick and Ellie Mace)

Let me repeat it: 'To stimulate your interest in and enthusiasm for the study of the arts, and to provide a foundation for further more detailed study at post-foundation level.' Now the second part of that statement is pretty straightforward. We are all familiar with clichés about 'not being able to run until you can walk'. If, then, you personally find parts of this foundation course less appealing than other parts, remember that what we are doing is providing you with a basic grounding in all the disciplines so that you are properly prepared to embark on the more specialized work at second and later levels.

However, the first part of Aim 1 is perhaps not quite so easily dealt with. To talk of 'stimulating interest and enthusiasm' may sound pretentious, or presumptuous, or may suggest that there is a place ready and waiting for us in Pseuds Corner of *Private Eye*. I'd like you for a moment just to reflect on why you are doing an arts foundation course as distinct, say, from a science, or a technology, or a social science foundation course. There are all sorts of possible reasons and, above all, possible *mixtures* of reasons. Just to get the ball rolling, I am going to suggest four possible approaches to the question of why one should be studying the arts.

1 You could (let's be honest about this) argue that the arts are a 'soft option' compared with Science or Maths, and that you are embarking on the Arts because that is the area in which you are most likely to be successful.

2 You could say that you are doing the arts because you find them 'enjoyable': you respond to poetry, you like reading novels, you are moved by music, you find reading about the past fascinating.

3 You may believe that if you are to have any real understanding of the universe, the world, and the society in which you live, you need to understand the artistic activities of human beings and appreciate their past achievements.

4 However, let's face it, you may really believe that the arts are a bit of 'a waste of time' compared, say, with other pursuits such as science or investing in the Stock Exchange.

There are four possible broad approaches. Now I am going to stop and ask you to do a little work.

EXERCISE

Read each of the following statements about the arts and indicate (by noting the appropriate number against each) which of the four approaches they roughly correspond to. In some cases you may feel that they overlap two approaches, in which case put down two numbers. In some cases you may feel that just noting down a number is not really a sufficient answer; if so scribble some extra comment expressing your doubts and difficulties.

(a) Great art, great music, and great writing move us by the deep insight which each gives into the human condition.

(b) The level of artistic and literary achievement is a measure of a country's level of civilization.

(c) The arts are confined to a minority; the majority struggle for the very barest existence: it is the struggles of the majority that should concern us.

(d) We can only understand the extent of human achievement if we understand mankind's endeavours in the arts, thought, and politics.

(e)   Science is about the future which is alive; the arts are about the past which is dead.

(f)   'Science: all these damned equations!'

(g)   'I've always done arts subjects.'

(h)   'I'd rather be a good student of the arts than a lousy science student.'

(i)   Only through knowledge can we find freedom: knowledge of man's artistic activities is as important as an understanding of science and technology.

(j)   'You've got to specialize in something: the arts are what I like best and what I do best.'

(k)   'I'm not an educated person if I don't appreciate the great works of art and literature.'

(l)   'Of my top ten "greats" of all time, two are scientists, two are statesmen, one is a philosopher, two are musicians, one is a dramatist, one a novelist, and one a painter.'

SPECIMEN ANSWER

(a)   I think the main point here is about the 'the real understanding' attainable through art, though there is perhaps also a sense of the arts, in a rather profound way, being 'enjoyable'. I'd put a 3 first, but probably also a 2.

(b)   This, I think, falls firmly in category 3.

(c)   At first sight this may seem to be a clear 4, art as 'a waste of time'. But the sort of note you might have scribbled here could have read: 'But if we are to be concerned with the struggles of the majority that certainly implies a knowledge of history, which is one of the arts subjects.' Beyond that, if you are really thinking this one through, you might have added something like this: 'But why is it that the arts are confined to a minority? Only through a study of the arts can we investigate this problem properly'.

(d)   This is clearly in category 3.

(e)   The implication of this, with the contrast between 'alive' and 'dead', rather is that of 4, the arts as 'waste of time'.

(f)   Here we have the suggestion that science is too difficult, and of approach 1, the arts as a 'soft option'.

(g)   This is approach 1 again, thought I suppose there could also be some suggestion of 2, finding the arts 'enjoyable'.

(h)   This also suggests a mixture of approaches 1 and 2, with the emphasis perhaps on the 'soft option' idea.

(i)   This is another version of approach 3.

(j)   The main emphasis of this, I think, is equally spread between approaches 1 and 2. However, there may be the implication too, that to achieve under-standing some kind of specialization is necessary, so there is perhaps an element of approach 3 here too.

(k)   This is essentially approach 3, though I suppose there could be an element of 2 if one thinks of education as in itself 'enjoyable'.

(l)   This is a bit of a phoney one – I hope you won't go around compiling top ten lists of great men. However, what it is saying is that a majority of the greats fall within the category of the arts and is therefore in effect supporting approach 3.

DISCUSSION

You'll be getting exercises of this sort throughout your correspondence texts. It is not here so much a matter of getting 'right' or 'wrong' answers; what I have been trying to do is to get you to think a little bit about the possible reasons for studying, or not studying, the arts.

However, you are still at the very beginning of this course: if by the end of it you have some clearer ideas of your own about the importance of studying the Arts, then we shall have succeeded in the first part of Aim 1.

There is one point about the first part of Aim 1 that I want to stress. Note that we speak of 'interest in and enthusiasm for the *study* of the arts'. Perhaps you do already respond directly to great works of literature, art or music; what is important in this university course is that you think about your responses, learn to analyse how works of art make their impact, and discuss how they relate to each other and to the society which created them. It's not going to be a matter of 'I know what I like', but rather of 'Now I can explain why I like some art better than other art, how certain particular developments in the arts came about, how they are related to the other arts and to the society of the time'.

EXERCISE

Turn now to the first page of colour plates in your A101 *Colour Supplement*. Note carefully the factual information which is given about each plate. Now answer the following questions:

1   Looking purely at the two paintings, and ignoring the printed factual information, state (a) one obvious similarity between the two paintings (b) two obvious differences between the two paintings.

2   From the factual information provided try to explain these two differences.

3   There is a further difference between the two paintings, not terribly obvious from the reproductions here, but made clear in the factual information. What is that?

4   Can you make any comment on the significance of the (?) in the factual information?

5   Are there any other comments you can make elaborating upon the contrasts between the two paintings? (I don't really expect you to have any more to say at this stage; but here is your big chance if you have!)

6   Which painting do you prefer? Give some reasons.

SPECIMEN ANSWERS

1   (a)   Both are landscapes.

(b)   The obvious difference, which I hope you did get, is that the first painting is representational or 'realistic', the second painting, much more in the twentieth-century idiom, is not quite an exact photographic representation of its subject. The second point, which you may perhaps not have got, is that the first painting contains two human figures, whereas the second painting, a much wider scene, does not contain any human beings at all.

2   I hope you were able to give an explanation for the first difference: obviously, the first painting was done at a time when 'realistic', representational, painting, was the accepted convention; by the time of the second painting, 1924, artistic conventions had changed considerably and representational painting is the exception rather than the rule. That's terribly simply put, but I think it's all we can do on the basis of the few brief words of factual information offered to us. The second difference may not have been so easy to deal with. I would put it like this: the first painting, described as a *romantic landscape*,

belongs, though quite properly you may well not be aware of this, to that period in history (which we shall be studying in this course) often known as 'the era of romanticism', and by placing these two figures, with their reflections in the pool, in this wooded landscape, the painter undoubtedly gives an evocative, romantic effect. That sort of effect, I think, is notably missing from the Kokoschka painting, which belongs to the notably 'unromantic' era of the 1920s.

3   It is clear from the text, if not from the reproductions themselves (as of course it would be clear if you had the original paintings in front of you) that the first painting is a watercolour, the second painting an oil.

4   The significance of the (?) is quite simply that art historians are not completely certain that Francis Danby was indeed the painter of this picture. This brings out an important point. In the arts there are a lot of things that we are not always completely sure about. Vital evidence is often missing. So be ready *not* to be given a set of propositions or a series of equations to memorize.

5   I don't know whether you added anything here or not. I really just asked the question to give me the opportunity to give an example of the sort of comment which, as you progress with your studies, you too will learn to make. It is that the small-scale *watercolour* belongs to a particular nineteenth-century British tradition, compared with the large-scale oil painting by Kokoschka which belongs to the mainstream of European painting.

6   Frankly, I think it's pretty difficult to pronounce on the basis of these two reproductions. My own judgement, I would have to admit, is really based upon what I know about the actual paintings. The first painting I find pleasant, but limited, and in its perhaps over-deliberate romanticism, very slightly twee. Kokoschka (who, by the way, became domociled in this country), I recognize as an important twentieth-century European painter. I see this as an ambitious work of both innovation and personal vision. If one is forced to make a judgement between, in fact, two rather unlike pieces of art, I have to prefer the Kokoschka.(Maybe I should add that, as a historian, my subject is the twentieth century, not the early nineteenth century: perhaps that affects my judgement as well.)

STUDY NOTE 1 (by Ellie Mace)

1   Introduction

For many of you this booklet, often referred to as a text or 'unit', is not only an introduction to A101 and university work generally, but also your first experience of learning from correspondence material. So in order to help you work through the unit we decided to include Study Notes. The Notes contain discussion of some issues that emerge from the text itself, and so they are included at the appropriate points in the text. They are not meant to give you a blueprint for how to study nor do they form a comprehensive account of 'study skills'. By using examples from the text to demonstrate some of the skills you will need (such as reading set books and making notes) I hope to help you start thinking in a *realistic* way about how you are going to tackle your work for this course, and encourage you to start experimenting with various approaches straight away. You will find advice of a more general kind (how to organize your time, how to use libraries and so on) in Open University publications such as *How to Study* and *Preparing to Study** which should have been sent to you by now. Although

*The plan is to withdraw both these publications in 1982 and replace them by a first year student's handbook which, among other things, will contain general advice about study techniques.

the advice contained in this unit is by contrast fairly specific, geared to the demands of this unit and this course, I hope that it will be useful to you for future work in the Arts.

I should emphasize at once that these Notes simply provide a starting point. You cannot learn overnight to 'select relevant material, interpret it and express yourself in good English prose' (in the words of the Second Aim of the course). The acquisition of these skills is a gradual process, central to the process of learning itself and part and parcel of a university education. You cannot learn such skills merely by reading about how to do them. You need to practise them. In one or two of the Study Notes I shall suggest some exercises to get you started.

2 Reading the Correspondence Texts

These texts are not sacrosanct and should not be seen as containing the Whole Truth. Neither, on the other hand, should they be approached as 'light' reading matter. While you are not expected to learn, in the sense of committing to memory, all or even much that you read, neither do we envisage you closing the text with a yawn and a stretch before snuggling down for the night. Correspondence texts are more like work books. We hope you will work through them in a *critical* frame of mind – asking yourself whether you really understand what the author is saying, whether you agree with it, how it fits in with the work you have done so far – continually testing your own ideas and experiences against those of the unit author. You'll find that in most units the authors set exercises or ask questions that they want you to stop and think about. Often they will ask you to write down your ideas or 'answers'. And sometimes you'll be asked to break off your study of the text to read extracts or chapters from set books. If you take these suggestions seriously you'll find it much easier to sustain a critical stance towards what you read. And you are unlikely to find that such exercises 'interrupt' your study of the text, but rather that they are aspects of your week's work as rewarding of time and effort as any other. (Indeed, I think you will find that working hard at some exercises, such as those that guide you through set book reading, is particularly rewarding. I shall have more to say about this later on.)

Perhaps this emphasis on being critical and testing out your own ideas strikes you as something someone like me is bound to say, while your own experience, or what other students say, leads you to think that you're more likely to succeed if you simply reproduce the 'messages' of the units in suitably disguised form. You might indeed succeed in terms of passing your courses. And you will no doubt learn quite a lot. But it won't be learning of the kind I am talking about. We (that is to say both Arthur Marwick and myself) shall be taking this a good deal further in Section 2 of this unit, so at this point I'll just put the matter rather baldly. The point of a course of academic study is not so much to acquire 'knowledge' in the sense of remembering all that you read, but rather to develop a fairly sophisticated network of *ideas* which will enable you to analyse problems put to you, and also to learn to use the available facts in the service of a particular line of argument – selecting among them and recognizing those that are relevant and telling. Since we are talking about developing ideas, frameworks for thinking, you can be successful only to the extent that you are prepared to make the effort to understand what you are reading as you go along and to think hard about it afterwards. Most of the exercises and questions in the text are designed to help you do this.

How you actually tackle the correspondence material is pretty well up to you. Some people work through a unit slowly, completing exercises and set book reading as they go along. Others prefer to read it through quickly (or 'skim' it) to get their bearings, and then go on to a second, more thorough, reading. With this first unit we think you should experiment a bit to see what approach suits you best.

3   *Getting Started*

Did you try to answer the questions Arthur Marwick asked on pp. 7–8 and p. 9? These exercises are, of course, optional – no-one can possibly know whether you stopped and considered the questions or whether you turned straightaway to Arthur Marwick's discussions of them. If you did attempt answers you may have felt that they were slight, or badly expressed, compared to his – you may not even have attempted them from fear that this would be the case. The good news is that no one can possibly know how 'bad' your answers are either!

As I've said already, such exercises are included to help you understand what you are reading as you go along, and to encourage you to think out your own views. If you jot down your answers to such questions along with any related thoughts you might have about them you will also be making a written record of some of your ideas. You can then draw on these notes when you come to write TMAs and when you want to revise the course. But perhaps most important of all at this stage is that by putting pen to paper you are taking the plunge into the course. However imperfect you feel your understanding is and however inadequate your answers, you are making the attempt. If you continue to do so you will make progress. If you hold back, thinking that at a later stage you'll 'know' more and be in a better position to produce polished answers, I predict that you'll be in for a disappointment.

Finally, two further points that arise from these particular exercises. First, occasionally the author may ask a question that you feel you can't possibly answer. (Sometimes he will even say he doesn't expect you to be able to, as Arthur Marwick does with regard to Q. 5 on p. 9). Sometimes the idea is to present something very challenging or mind-stretching. But often it is because there are one or two points, perhaps incidental to the theme but nonetheless important or illuminating, that the author can make fairly briefly in answer to questions but which couldn't be introduced in the main body of the text given the necessary limits on the discussion. So try not to feel depressed because you can't answer such questions, or irritated by the fact that they have been asked. Rather, concentrate on trying to understand the discussions of them. Second, you should not expect all the units to contain as many exercises as this one does. Although I have said that exercises are deliberately included in order actively to involve you in what you are studying, it is also true to say that they are only included where it is considered appropriate. In some units there may be long sections of text containing no exercises at all. More often than not this will be because the author is trying to develop a fairly involved argument, or introduce you to a difficult concept or set of ideas, by means of explanation and examples, followed by further explanation and so on. In these cases, exercises are only appropriate once the arguments are complete or the concepts fully explored. (And it will probably take you some time to show that you have understood such arguments or concepts, so in all probability you would be asked to write about them in TMAs rather than as answers to questions in the texts.) You will find that most in-text exercises will take you perhaps ten or fifteen minutes to complete, with the exception of exercises that require you to read extracts from set books.

SECTION 1 (by Arthur Marwick) CONTINUED

EXERCISE

Now I want you to read three passages from your set book *Nature and Industrialization*. This is a fat volume which you've had to buy and which you're expected to use – not by reading from cover to cover but by selecting here and there extracts relevant to whatever you're working on at the time. Now read:

1   Extract XIX. 4 (p. 302), Jeremy Bentham on 'Self Interest', 1824;
2   Extract XVIII. 2 (p. 270), Karl Marx and Friedrich Engels on 'Communism', 1847 lines 1–18;
3   Extract XXV. 2 (p. 370), George Eliot on 'Gwendolen "desires to be independent"', 1874–76.

QUESTIONS

1 It could be said that each of these extracts belongs to a different one of the arts disciplines. Allocate each one to the appropriate discipline.
2 What argument is being advanced in this passage from Jeremy Bentham on 'Self Interest'?
3 What is the main point being put forward in these first eighteen lines of the Communist Manifesto?
4 It could be said that in this passage Gwendolen is 'learning a lesson'; what lesson is that?

SPECIMEN ANSWERS

1 The Bentham extract is from a piece of philosophical writing and therefore could be said to belong to philosophy. The Communist Manifesto is a particular type of historical document and therefore could be said to belong to the study of history. *Daniel Deronda* is a novel, and therefore this extract could be said to belong to literature. In fact, as this foundation course is designed to demonstrate (that is the Fourth Aim which we shall come to shortly) the divisions are not as rigid as that: many philosophers are interested in the study of Marxism, a historian might well have something to say about both Bentham and George Eliot and her novel. For the moment, I hope you will agree that the first two passages are both, at the very least, provocative, and that the third passage immediately arouses our interest and sympathy.

2 That self interest is the basis of human action.

3 Communism is so important that Communists should now put forward their own manifesto.

4 That her life as a well-off young lady has in no way prepared her for the tasks of earning her own living.

STUDY NOTE 2: SET READING (by Ellie Mace)

The exercise you have just done is an example of what I described earlier: you had to stop working through the unit and read some extracts from one of your set books. You were then asked some questions about the extracts. (I think you should have written down your answers, though you were not explicitly asked to do so, because it forces you to read more carefully and think harder about what precisely you want to say.) The task here is to discover how best to tackle such reading.

As you know, Arthur Marwick asked you some questions about the extracts he directed you to read. It is a good idea to look at such questions *before* you get down to your reading so that you can bear them in mind as you read. You will then have some idea about what you might get out of an extract, chapter or whatever. I do not mean to say that you should mentally rule out any points that do not have a direct bearing on questions you have been asked, just that such questions provide a focus for your first encounter with the reading matter. In the case of reading related to TMA work, the question you have been set will provide a similar focus. But whether you have this kind of help or not you will often have to decide for yourselves what is significant.

If you are tackling a book you might first look at the index or contents page to get a rough idea of its scope and then read the descriptions of the contents of those chapters that seem to be relevant, along with chapter summaries, if they are provided. It is a good idea to 'skim' through the relevant chapters fairly quickly just to check that they do seem to contain the kind of thing you're after. You can then get down to reading them more slowly and carefully. Whatever you are reading, article, chapter or book, you have to try to pick out, and make sure you understand, the author's *main* points or lines of argument and try to distinguish between them and what is illustrative of, or incidental to, them. You should ask yourselves the same questions that I suggested you ask about correspondence texts – whether what you are reading makes sense to you, how it ties in with what has gone before, what it might lead to – and so force yourselves really to get to grips with what the author is trying to say. You will want to make some notes of the author's main points and your own reflections on what you have read, and you will have to give some thought to how you are going to use this material. I will take up both these points in later Notes. If you feel you urgently need practice in distilling the essence from what you read, you might suggest to your tutor-counsellor that some time be set aside for it at a tutorial session.

2 THE SECOND AIM OF THE COURSE
(by Ellie Mace and Arthur Marwick)

2.1 (By Ellie Mace)

Just to remind you, this aim reads: 'To help you develop the basic skills of clear and logical thinking, and of selecting relevant material, interpreting it, and expressing yourself in good English prose and to introduce you to what is meant by education and the learning process at university level'. In an earlier Study Note I suggested that learning at university level is more a matter of developing networks of ideas about a subject, and learning how to analyse a problem, than of memorizing a lot of facts about it. I think if we examine the last part of the aim first you will understand rather better what we mean by this, and what we mean by talk about 'skills' like 'clear and logical thinking'. Notice that I have written the word 'skills' in inverted commas. This is because 'clear and logical thinking' are skills of a kind, but I don't want you to think in terms of anything mechanical. We do not mean to suggest that you can learn a set of rules and put them into practice, or that there is anything like a blue-print for 'clear thinking'. Rather, the aim tries to encapsulate the ingredients of particular habits of thinking and a way of approaching issues and problems that are generally referred to as 'academic'.

If you listen to academic debate of the kind you will come across in some of the TV and radio programmes for this course you'll find that the people concerned are far less interested in forcing their opinions upon each other, or regaling each other with the 'facts' of the matter, than they are in developing particular lines of argument. They will explain both their point of view and their reasons for holding it carefully, and possibly at some length. They will give each other the time necessary to develop a particular argument and try to understand each other's point of view by listening to it carefully. And they try to make sure they are understanding each other by asking what precisely is meant by certain words and phrases. This is because lines of argument that lay bare the *reasons* for people holding the views they do are more important to academics than those views or conclusions by themselves.*

For example, some people believe that abortion is morally wrong. Others disagree. But there are various reasons for taking either view and a number of possible positions, or lines of argument, for and against each. People who believe abortion to be wrong will probably do so because they think it is wrong to take life. But they will have to say something about what they mean by 'life', or the scope they will allow the term. One person may allow it a broad scope and so conclude that not only is it wrong to abort, but also to kill animals. Another person might be referring more narrowly to human life, involving the further assumption that a foetus is a human being. Yet another might take a middle path claiming that what is wrong is the taking of human or potential human life, assuming the foetus potentially to be a human being. Similarly, although arguments 'for' abortion might well be based on the notion that people have certain rights (in particular the right to freedom), they could still take many different forms. One person might stress the right of freedom to determine what happens to one's own body, with reference to the right to health and to refuse surgery if one wishes. Another might take up the freedom to live one's own life happily, unencumbered either by an unwanted child or the guilt of having produced one. Yet another might pursue the right to freedom of choice, and the position of the individual *vis à vis* the state. The point is that until we know precisely what line

---

*I am grateful to Rosalind Hursthouse for her help with this section of the text – in particular with the debate which follows and for providing the analogy with chess later on.

15

people are taking – until we understand the beliefs and assumptions that under-lie their positions (their *reasons* for believing that abortion is 'right' or 'wrong') – discussion can't really take off and any kind of agreement or resolution is pre-sumably out of the question. This is why academic argument often begins with a kind of 'ground-clearing': the attempt to understand each other by listening carefully and, above all, by asking questions about each other's meaning which often result in agreement to proceed in certain ways – to leave on one side issues that are not central or potentially fruitful to the discussion, for example. The point of such questioning is not to 'score' off one another, or to parade insights and knowledge, and nor should it be seen as 'nit-picking'. (I am not, of course, claiming that academics *never* do these things: they are after all only human – whatever that means!). Rather, the process reveals that many of the terms in which we express our beliefs (such as 'life', above) can be defined, and are understood in different ways by different people. Only by careful and sym-pathetic probing can both parties come to a better understanding of what each other means to say, what issues are involved, what it is that divides them, and why. It is the way people approach a problem, the way they analyse it and argue about it, that we label 'academic' or 'non-academic', not their conclusions.

This kind of debate is the very opposite of 'typical' bar-room conversation in which a question like' 'What do you think of this mob we've got running things then?' invites an equally aggressive, and possibly more colourful, reply one way or the other. Whether the outcome is happy accord or a ding-dong battle of wits, both parties are likely to feel better for it. In this context it would be quite inappropriate for the listener to enquire into which 'things' the speaker might have in mind, ponder over the extent to which the government might be said to 'run' these things (perhaps bearing in mind the role of the civil service), or draw the speaker's attention to the use of the word 'mob' which might be seen as an attempt to push the listener in a certain direction! Of course I am exaggerating. I do not mean either to criticize 'typical' bar-room conversation or to suggest that academic discussion is never conducted in bars. And I imagine that few academ-ics would conduct themselves in this way. The serious point is that such discus-sion has a different function and takes a different form from academic debate, and each has its place. In this course you are required to approach issues con-nected with the arts in an academic way.

In academic debate <u>conclusions</u> depend on analysis and argument that has gone before; one arrives at or reaches a conclusion. So just as we might find an academic argument unconvincing because we disagree with the beliefs incorpo-rated in it or upon which it rests (as in the case of abortion, for example), so we might also criticize an academic argument because the conclusions do not seem to follow from the foregoing analysis. Or because we suspect that in order to 'arrive at' a particular conclusion the argument has been suitably tailored – points, or evidence, that tend to suggest a different conclusion have been glos-sed over or ignored. When we criticize an argument in this way we are, of course, taking a rather detached view of things and this too is a feature of academic debate. It arises out of the fact that certain aspects of argument in general – for example, making logical connections, being consistent, seeing where an argument is leading – are skills that people can acquire if they care enough to practise them. This word 'care' perhaps raises what looks like a paradox. I've suggested that academics 'care', and yet earlier I described a situa-tion in which two people with very different views could be detached enough to sit down and agree about how they might go on to argue about them. Academic debate sometimes does strike people as a kind of game played apparently for its own sake, without passion and even without commitment to any one point of view. For example, two people might take up contrary 'positions' and try out arguments on each other to see how far they can go unchecked. Player A may even offer player B a stronger argument against A's own case than B seems able to provide – rather like one player in a game of chess saying to the other 'If you make that move I'll win in three moves – wouldn't you like to take it back and makes this one instead?' But I think this just underlines what I said earlier about the lines of argument people develop being more important than the conclu-

16

sions they reach. To it I would add that the *way* these lines of argument are developed and pursued is what really counts. In the next unit Ossie Hanfling discusses many of the, often rather subtle, ways in which people 'cheat' in argument and so manipulate the beliefs of the reader or listener. Often people don't set out to do this deliberately. But it is because academics think that the problems they try to deal with are important, they 'care' about them, that they believe in dealing with them as honestly as they can. As I said before this means that they must try to examine the beliefs and assumptions that underlie their views by making them accessible to others – open to scrutiny and criticism. (This is one of the reasons for the emphasis in the academic world on publising one's work.) They must also play by the 'rules' of argument even when they care passionately about what they are presenting (which, perhaps contrary to popular belief, they often do). And, among other things, this means recognizing and attempting to confront arguments that run counter to their own and not just brushing them aside; attempting to deal with evidence to the contrary, not discounting it and certainly not producing false 'evidence' to support their own cases.

The problems academics try to deal with are important in another sense too. They are *problems*. This means that they have not yet been resolved (if indeed such problems are open to final solution, as many issues in the arts are not). But it is rarely the case that people have not thought about them before. So whatever one's own view there are likely to be strong arguments against it. 'Education and the learning process at university level' means, among other things, coming to understand the positions people have taken in the past, being able to recognize the strength and relevance of certain arguments to any given position, in support of or in opposition to it, and being able to perceive what is at stake. Just as skilful chess players can recognize and appreciate their opponent's moves as well as their own, can think of good moves for the opponents as well as for themselves, so people skilled at academic debate can recognize and appreciate their opponents' evidence and arguments and can think of relevant evidence and good arguments for their oponents' view as well as for their own. A further point of the analogy is this: just as chess players can practise by playing against themselves so we can develop our academic skills by practising putting a good case for a view we do not believe in, as well as for a view that we do support. The outcome is the same as I described earlier: it makes us clearer about our own position and we understand better what issues are involved, what it is that may divide us from others, and why. Enlargement of mind and enrichment of view is the name of this particular 'game'. Which, finally, brings me face to face with the issue of winning and losing.

My remarks so far may suggest an essentially 'British' outlook: what counts is not whether you won or lost, but how you played the game! I don't want to go back on that but I would like to qualify it somewhat. Of course when people believe something strongly they want to demonstrate to others that they are 'right' and to persuade those who disagree with them to change their minds. Academics are not different from anyone else in this respect, and persuasion is part and parcel of their enterprise. In this sense they, too, want to 'win'. (But they shouldn't want to win at all costs – at the cost of any of the forms of dishonesty I described earlier for example.) Indeed, academics may be some of the world's most reluctant losers: they take a good deal of persuading. This is understandable, I think, given that a lot of time, effort and hard thinking will have gone into the formation and formulation of their views. But it does raise a question: if people are unlikely to change their views as a result of debate or discussion, what is the point of it all? Is it, after all, just a game, a sterile exercise, an ego-trip? It will come as no surprise to you that I think the answer to the second question is, no. A person's present view will have been formed partly through discussion and argument in the past. People do change their minds, albeit gradually and piecemeal. (Though occasionally a particularly intense or unusual experience can lead to a 'revolution' in a person's thinking – such has even been claimed in the columns of *Sesame* for the effects of OU courses and summer schools!) Furthermore, when people continue to be prepared to listen to and consider the other point of view, their minds are at least open to the possibility of change. They have not made up their minds 'once and for all'. Even quite small concessions made here and there in argument can lead to quite dramatic changes of mind over a fairly long period.

Coming down to earth, you may be thinking that at this stage in your career your problem is more likely to be how to reach a conclusion at all! Rather than thinking of yourself as one of two 'disputants' in a debate, you may find it more helpful to imagine yourself as a detached third party listening to both sets of views, trying to weigh them up and decide on their relative merits and finally coming to your own considered opinion. The arguments you 'listen' to will in reality be drawn largely from correspondence texts and set books, but the way you interpret them and the conclusions you reach should be your own. This is why in earlier Study Notes I emphasized the importance of reading carefully and in a critical frame of mind, of testing your own ideas against those that you read about, and asking whether or not you agree with what is being said. Unless you do this you simply will not be able to reach any conclusions at all. However, as I've said, reaching a conclusion is rarely a simple 'yes/no' 'right/wrong' affair, and it does not involve making up one's mind once and for all. A conclusion to a discussion of abortion, for example, might be 'So on the whole I conclude that abortion is wrong, but perhaps in certain cases a greater wrong would be done by denying a woman the right to it'. But this is to anticipate things: the *first* stage of the whole process is being able to read or listen to something carefully and pick out the *main* points the author or speaker is making. It helps to be able to express them quite briefly and simply. Try it now.

EXERCISE

Here is a piece of dialogue from this week's television programme, 'Why the Humanities?'. W. H. Auden, the distinguished poet, is being interviewed by Patrick Garland.

Auden: A poet *qua poet* [that is, 'a poet *as a* poet'] has only one political duty, whatever attitude he has as a citizen and that is by his own example to defend the purity of the language against its constant corruption.

Garland: You don't think that it can have a more active influence than that.

Auden: I think one would have to say that the history and political and social history of Europe would be what it has been if Dante cum Shakespeare, Goethe, Titian, Michelangelo, Mozart, Beethoven had never lived. We'd have missed an awful lot of fun. (Laughter) I mean, there are people of course who have influenced certain courses of history, I mean like Voltaire or Rousseau and so on. They're not sort of pure artists in that sense.

1   In a sentence or two say as clearly as you can, and in simple language, what point(s) you think Auden is making.

2   Do you agree with him? Give one or two reasons for your answer. (Just jot them down in your notebook without worrying about how you put them. We'll return to this later on.)

ANSWER

Auden argues that pure artists have had no influence on political and social history. He believes that the artist's only duty, as an artist, is to his/her art.

DISCUSSION

If your 'answer' wasn't very close to mine don't worry about it too much. These issues will be discussed later on and you'll be able to think about them again then. I don't of course know what you said in answer to the second question –

'Do you agree?' When we return to the topic you'll be presented with a lot of ideas about it and it will be interesting to see if your views change as a result. So keep for comparison what you have written this time round.

The first part of the second aim of the course stresses the importance of clear and logical thinking. Unit 2B is specially designed to help you develop such skills, as also is Unit 9 together with brief passages which you will find at the end of various units throughout the course. So I will confine myself to discussing clear and logical thinking from the point of view of how we express ourselves in writing. Here, as throughout this section of the text, it is not my intention to mystify or bewilder. I have tried to describe what it means to take an academic approach, what the purposes and goals of academics are, so that you are aware from the start what sort of community you have joined and what you might be working towards. None of what I have described can be achieved overnight – and this is perhaps particularly true of learning to write well. Because your arguments will be presented in writing, you have to be prepared to spend quite a lot of your time learning how to answer the questions you have been asked in 'good English prose', particularly if this is your first OU course. Many of you will not need reminding of this because you are probably quite worried enough about it already. While I do not want you to underestimate how important it is, it is nevertheless true that the most fluent and engaging style of writing cannot disguise failure to get to grips with the question you have been asked, incomplete understanding of what you have read, or just plain confusion. Writing can appear muddled for a number of different reasons, separately or together.

1   *What you have written is simply irrelevant to the question you have been asked.* This could be because you haven't understood the question itself. But the fact that you've missed the point completely usually suggests that you haven't got to grips with the topic at all. If you have understood what you have studied in your units and set books you will know what the most important issues are, you will be aware of the main arguments for and against various propositions and, above all, you will see the significance of what is being said, what the *point* of it all is. This is what it means to understand something. To take a fairly straightforward example: if you were asked to write an essay presenting a case for and against abortion and to discuss the implications of each position, you would have to do three things,
(a)   give a case for abortion,
(b)   give a case against abortion.
You would, we are supposing, have read these arguments in the correspondence units or set books. If you presented the main planks of each, fully and accurately, you would have done well. If you could also see ways of strengthening the arguments, or could think of arguments of your own, all the better.
(c)   Discuss the implications of (a) and (b).
At this point you are called upon to interpret what you have read and show that you have read it carefully and critically. You will begin to reveal your own judgements and point of view by the way in which you argue against the assumptions of one case and criticize its consequences, and defend the assumptions and consequences of the other against possible objections. (And incidentally I would say that you should spend at least half your time on this part of your essay answer.) If you spent all your time simply describing the cases for and against abortion, you would be accused of missing the point or of failing to answer the question – the cases have to be related to each other and weighed up. If, instead of presenting (a) and (b) as coherent lines of argument you simply wrote down a number of disjointed statements relating to either side (a Christian might say . . . but then a feminist would say; outlawing abortion leads to back-street abortions, but on the other hand legalizing it leads to a crisis of conscience for some doctors), you would not have answered the question, for you would not have *presented a case* for and against abortion. If moved, say, by sincere belief or personal experience, you spent the whole time describing how you feel about abortion, you would be accused not only of not answering the question but also of adopting an entirely inappropriate ('unacademic') approach to the subject.

19

2   What you have written is not entirely off the point but is somewhat garbled in places.
This is a far less serious problem. Most of you will find that you get into a
muddle sometimes. Your mind is not a complete blank on any subject and when
you go through the process of trying to make connections between your existing
thoughts and the new ideas that are being presented to you, you are bound to
feel confused at times. Your tutors understand this and try to help you by their
comments on your essays, and discussions at the study centre. However, when
you are presenting other people's arguments I need hardly stress that it is
important to take the trouble to get them right. Often you are asked to summarize a person's views as a starting point for discussion in an essay. The first step
towards producing such a summary is to pick out only those points that are
relevant to the question you have been asked. I'd like you to practise this first
stage now.

EXERCISE

Turn again to the Jeremy Bentham passage on 'Self Interest'. What *exceptions* to
his theory of self interest does Bentham admit? (Arthur Marwick summarized
this theory on p. 13: 'self interest is the basis of human action').

SPECIMEN ANSWER

1   People under strong stimulus or excitement ('ebullitions').

2   Persons affected by some domestic or private tie (family relationship, friend-
ship, or love, for instance).

3   The tiny minority of politically-committed people who do put public interest
before individual interest.

DISCUSSION

I hope you didn't find it difficult to isolate the first two exceptions (though you
may have been undecided about the third) but if you did, I suggest you read the
extract again and see if you can make sense of it now. The next step would be to
express these points, and no others, in a connected sentence using your own
words as far as possible. I would include Bentham's third exception, for the sake
of completeness, though I would add the rider that he effectively rules these
people out as too few in number and anyway undistinguishable from the mass.
(By all means try your hand at this if you want to.)

*3   You have shown signs that you have grasped the question and understood what you
have read, but your own powers of expression sometimes cast doubt on this.* It is particularly galling if the quality of your thought is questioned because you cannot do
justice to it in writing. But what it means in academic terms is that other people
cannot gain access to your ideas, and for this reason you should be concerned to
improve your writing. Since your main aim is always to make your meaning
clear, you should try to express yourself in a simple, straightforward way. It is
mistaken to think that an academic argument has to be presented extremely
formally or elaborately, and sound 'high-powered'. The best writers often put
things so simply that they seem almost obvious. They appear to speak to you
directly, almost as they might in conversation: I say 'almost' because written
language is not the same as spoken language. In speech we use a kind of
'conversational short-hand' and a range of tones which we supplement by
appropriate facial expressions and bodily gestures. In writing however, we have
to take more care to strike the right note. What we say has to be able to stand on
its own and to bear scrutiny. But it still seems to me better to err in the direction
of a conversational style than to be pompous or condescending. Of course,
everyone would *like* to be able to write well so in a way it's rather insulting to say
something like 'write clearly and concisely' as though that is going to make all
the difference. In the end I think the only way actually to improve your writing
is to write a lot and be critical of what you write. So I am not going to say any

more about it now. You will have plenty of opportunity to write as you work through the course and many unit authors will offer you guidance. You'll find the detailed comments on your TMA scripts particularly helpful and you can always discuss any problems with your tutor-counsellor, and your fellow students, at the study centre.

2.2 (By Arthur Marwick)

I want to say something more about the second part of Aim 2 which reads 'to introduce you to what is meant by education and the learning process at university level.' In a way, a university *is* an unreal world. We set you questions on which we expect you to write essays when, of course, much of the information and many of the arguments which you put into these essays will already be well-known to those who are marking them. At the same time, we do hope that you will show a certain amount of original thought of your own, even although that thought is unlikely to strike your tutor as particularly striking. Perhaps there does seem to be an element of a game in all this. But the idea behind it is that all the time, you – the student – are continuing to *develop*. It is not a question of simply acquiring a certain number of facts, memorizing a particular list of names, nor even of acquiring a certain number of skills. When we speak of 'education and the learning process at university level' what we have in mind is that you, as members yourselves now of the university community, should steadily become able to think and exercise judgement, independently, but always in accordance with certain accepted standards of scholarship.

I expect that all sounds a bit high-flown. Here I shall just make some introductory comments on points which do sometimes puzzle students.

1   We are not interested in whether you can memorize something, we are interested in whether you *understand* it. For example, there would be no point at all memorizing the Auden conversation from the television programme (it is, naturally enough given the circumstances, in rather sloppy conversational style, not quite good enough for a written essay). What is important is to get at the main argument about artistic figures having no influence on political and social history, then to start *thinking* for yourself as to whether you actually agree with this argument, and, after that, with perhaps a little bit of reading, being in a position to present an interpretation of your own on the question of the artist's influence on history.

There is no point in memorizing the Bentham extract: the point is to understand the arguments and, again, to be able to present your own reactions to them. Ask yourself whether you agree with the premises of the argument, and (an entirely separate question) whether you think the argument is valid. You might note that, in talking about *every* human being Bentham is talking about you, so a personal response ('Yes I am like that' / 'No I am not.') is quite in order. But a personal response is no more than the beginning of assessing what is said. Philosophy aims to encourage a sort of judicious detachment and this involves working out how you could argue with someone whose personal response was different from yours.

In a novel as rich and subtle as *Daniel Deronda* there are all kinds of different points to be grasped apart from simply remembering the story: the language used, the techniques employed in presenting the narrative: note, for example, how in turn we feel deeply for the predicament of Gwendolen, then for the predicament of Herr Klesmer. But, now, on the question of memorizing facts. If you were studying *Daniel Deronda* you would have to know it well enough to remember the names of such leading characters as Gwendolen and Klesmer: otherwise you'd find great difficulty in writing intelligently about the book. Thus with *Jane Eyre* which is the set novel for this course. That's a good example: it's not the facts themselves that are vitally important, but without a certain mastery of the facts you will not be able to develop the arguments or demonstrate the critical understanding which we require.

2   Don't swallow arguments whole. Keep thinking, be critical of what you are reading. There are few simple truths in the arts. I was trying to illustrate this point in this week's television programme. You will remember that we showed an extract from the BBC further education programme *Mistress of Hardwick*. There I was saying that in reacting to a programme you should be asking yourself 'What kind of programme is it, what sort of audience is it designed for?' The major point I was making was that, excellent though the programme is on its own terms, it inevitably smooths out the difficulties of historical study: it has, in the time available, to present a neat little story. Actually, writing history is a rather painful business as you have to try to reconstruct the story from the evidence, much of it imperfect or even non-existent. It is part of 'the learning process at university level' to have a feel for the complexities of the subject: not to expect everything to be cut-and-dried, to be open to memorization like multiplication tables.

3   Your written assignments will be read by tutors who, obviously, will know a good deal more about the subject than you do. The best advice I can give is that you should write your essays as if you were aiming them at an intelligent friend. Do not, as has already been stressed, simply retail a list of tedious facts; but do at the same time include all the necessary information (even although it will already be well-known to your tutor) necessary to support the arguments you are putting forward. For all of your information, and most of your arguments, you will, of course, be dependent on your course units and other reading. But do not simply present a series of arguments and opinions: make it clear by the end of the essay where *you* stand on a particular topic.

4   So we come to the vexed question of plagiarism. Plagiarism means taking someone else's material and passing it off as your own. But since you're a student you will obviously get almost all of your material from your teachers, and from books. It really all comes back to my first point about *understanding*. Show that you have understood someone else's argument by, as it were, 'taking it over' and expressing it in your own words. What is being looked for all the time is some sign that you have been doing some thinking of your own: that you are not just regurgitating material presented to you. If you do feel like quoting directly the words of some author, then remember always to put these words in quotation marks. However, too many direct quotations begins to look like scissors-and-paste.

3 THE THIRD AIM OF THE COURSE
(by Arthur Marwick and John Ferguson)

INTRODUCTION (by Arthur Marwick)

This aim, remember, is 'to introduce you to the separate purposes and methods of the different individual disciplines in the Arts.' Once you have got through this Introduction, and have completed Unit 2B, the first one on clear and logical thinking (actually entitled 'Uses and Abuses of Argument') you will find that thereafter you go through a series of introductions, each lasting three weeks, to the different individual disciplines, starting off with history. Here we want to give you a quick overview, and comparison, of all the disciplines. First of all, John Ferguson discusses 'Music, The Visual Arts and Literature'.

MUSIC, THE VISUAL ARTS AND LITERATURE (by John Ferguson)

EXERCISE

Write down the most obvious thing which marks off each of these arts from the others.

(a) Music.
(b) Art – say, painting.
(c) Literature.

DISCUSSION

You may have written something subtle. Most obviously surely:

Music is heard.
Art is seen.
Literature may be heard (it ought to be heard more often than it is), or may be read with the eye: the most obvious difference from the others is that it uses words.

At first this seems to put literature apart from the others. Music is a pattern of sounds, art a pattern of shapes and colours, but the basic units of literature are words, which have more literal meanings. It is probably true to say that literature makes more obvious demands on the conscious use of the mind to analyse meaning than the others. But the demands are only more obvious, not necessarily bigger or stronger.

(a) It is tempting to suggest that in its simplest form to understand a piece of music you would ask what it sounds like. The British composer, Ralph Vaughan Williams (1872–1958), wrote a piece for violin and orchestra called *The Lark Ascending*. In this we hear the song of the lark imitated by the violin. In *On Hearing the First Cuckoo in Spring* by Frederick Delius (1862–1934) we hear an imitation of the cuckoo. In Prokofiev's *Peter and the Wolf* the oboe actually gives us the sound of a quacking duck (Prokofiev 1891–1953). But we soon realize that this is not the whole story. There is such a thing as imitative music: it is a form of 'programme music' – music written to a programme, as it were. But there is a lot to the Delius besides the cuckoo-call, and it would be a very dull work if there were not. So that we would have to say not that this music imitates the cuckoo, but that the composer is using sound to create in us the feelings he had when he heard the cuckoo. And with much music – say one of the forty-one symphonies by Mozart – it would be difficult to talk in these terms at all.

(b)   It is similarly tempting to suggest that in its simplest form to understand a painting you would ask what it looks like. All the town halls of the world have endless portraits of Mayor X and Mayor Y, and the most obvious point of them is to show what Mayor X and Mayor Y looked like. And yet they can't. For one thing they are flat canvases and Mayor X was fat; for another they are unmoving and Mayor Y was always on the move. More seriously, the more an artist concentrates on creating the illusion of what something or someone looked like, somehow the more trivial his picture seems to become. The great portrait painters have somehow conveyed not just what a person looked like but what he was like. One of the most frightening stories of genius is told of the Austrian painter Oskar Kokoschka (b. 1886). He painted a portrait which friends of the sitter did not consider a good likeness. Years later the sitter had a stroke and experienced a religious conversion; and the same friends came now to see in the portrait a true likeness. Kokoschka's supporters used to claim that he painted not the body but the soul; on this occasion he appears to have painted the latent qualities of the soul. So far from copying life, art had anticipated it. In landscape it is the same. Many landscapes evoke a mood rather than portraying a scene. John Constable (1776–1837) was for ever painting Dedham Vale in Suffolk. There is a striking church tower there, and he puts it in all sorts of places where the architect never put it. Why? Because besides saying, 'This is what Dedham looks like', he is also fulfilling his function as artist by expressing the arrangement of form and colour suggested to him by what he saw at Dedham. Some artists in the present century have indeed concentrated on form itself without representing the world around us at all.

(c)   It is similarly tempting to suggest that in its simplest form to understand a work of literature is to understand the words, to ask what it says. No harm in that. But it doesn't take you very far. This is most apparent in poetry, where there is obviously something beyond the unvarnished meaning of the words – order, rhythm, sound all count. The great Latin poet Horace (Quintus Horatius Flaccus, 65 BC–8BC) said, 'It is the succession and combination that really matters.' In prose too the early theorists made considerable study of rhythm, especially in its effect at the end of a sentence. It can be a powerful experience to listen to a sermon in Welsh, or a poem in Chinese, even if you do not understand a word of the language. Something is conveyed apart from the meaning of the words. Moreover, the words, *as they are used within the world of the poem*, can acquire implications which they don't possess as they're used in everyday language.

(d)   A difference is already clear. With nearly all literature there is an obvious meaning to the words, though something else as well. With most but not all painting we can say that it is in some sense 'representational', though that is not the whole story. But most music is in the obvious sense non-representational: the sound, so to speak, does not paint a picture.

We have passed (have we not?) from *meaning* to *form*, and in all three arts we see that it is not easy to separate what you have to say from the way that you say it. For this is what form is: the way you organize your expression, the pattern which shapes your work. This leads me to suggest to you four further thoughts.

(a)   The purest succession of sounds, the simplest visual image, and any word have some associations for us. To put it obviously. If you play two notes at an interval of a major third, the higher first, I cannot help thinking of a cuckoo (though Delius uses both maor and minor thirds). If you paint an orange circle I cannot help thinking of the sun. It is likely that such associations will be difficult to identify; they will be unconscious; but they will be there.

(b)   Such associations will sometimes be individual and personal. This is one reason why we never respond in exactly the same way to a work of art. A painting of the crucifixion will evoke a different response from a Christian, a Buddhist and a Marxist. But we are all human beings, and have a vast stock of common responses, and even more within a single culture. If this were not so, art could not communicate anything at all.

(c)   But of course the majority of music, and much art, does not proceed in the obvious sense from such associations, though I am not certain that it escapes them altogether.

(d)   It is important to realize that it is by no means true that an artist always thinks of what he wants to convey and then thinks of a form to put it in. The sculptor, Jacob Epstein (1880–1959), tells how he had in his studio a great block of marble for months before he gradually saw how his *Genesis* might emerge from it. The marble was there before the subject, and the form and meaning took shape in his mind together and inseparably. Similarly, the novelist Joseph Conrad (1857–1924) said 'some kind of moral discovery should be the object of every tale'. Without pressing the word 'moral' at present, we can note that he regards the creation of a work of art as a process of discovery. It is in the course of grappling with this 'subject' that the writer discovers what it actually is.

Figure 1   Epstein, Genesis, *1931 (From Sir Jacob Epstein,* An Autobiography, *Vista Books, 1963, 2nd ed. Reproduced by courtesy of Hon. Sir Clive Bossom and Vista Books)*

I want you now to think further about the differences between the arts. I am going to simplify things a little by taking poetry (instead of all literature), painting (instead of all visual art), and music.

QUESTION

Through what organ of the body does each make its appeal to the mind?

DISCUSSION

Painting through the eye, music through the ear. What did you say about poetry? I think the answer must be, through the ear, though we often in fact read with the eye without reading aloud. But we should surely be 'hearing' the sound inside us. (I don't myself think that this is always true of prose.) Similarly a musician may read a score with his eye, but he will be hearing the sound in his mind.

QUESTION

What are the ingredients which the poet uses to make a poem, the painter for a picture, the musician for a composition?

DISCUSSION

The poet uses words to make phrases or sentences. (Notice that sometimes in 'using' them he gives them new meanings: he makes them new.) The words and phrases they make have meanings; their arrangement produces effects through sound and rhythm and form. Words and phrases create images which stimulate the imagination.

> And Pity, like a naked newborn babe,
> Striding the blast, or heaven's cherubim, horsed
> Upon the sightless couriers of the air,
> Shall blow the horrid deed in every eye. . . .

(Shakespeare, *Macbeth*)

The painter puts paint on a canvas, obviously. In one sense these are his ingredients; in another they are colour and shape or form. The musician uses sounds; these may be arranged in sequence to produce a tune, and together to produce harmony. Rhythm and form are essential ingredients of a piece of music.

Notice one thing that marks off a work of art from the 'real world. It is strictly limited in time and space. Even if it sprawls across vast areas and extents of time, like Wagner's *The Ring of the Nibelung* or Berlioz's *The Trojans* or Tolstoy's *War and Peace* or Browning's *The Ring and the Book*, it is still finite. Think of a typical landscape painting in an art gallery. The scene the painter saw wasn't rectangular, and physically he did not see it as rectangular. A sonneteer distils an experience into fourteen lines, a writer of japanese *haiku* distils it into seventeen syllables. All art sets itself limits, and works selectively.

There are two obvious points each of which marks off one of these three arts we have been discussing from the other two. The poet uses words, and words have a meaning which a blob of colour or a sound do not have. The painter produces a work which you can see in a single instant: a poem or piece of music has to be experienced over a period of time. These are valid distinctions, but they are not, I think, absolute.

QUESTION

Can you see how the ingredients of a painting or piece of music may have meaning much as a word has meaning, and how a painting may be experienced sequentially?

DISCUSSION

We have in fact touched on this earlier. To take a simple example. The word 'sun' is associated for us with a celestial object. A round blob of reddish gold paint may have the same association. The word 'cuckoo' is associated for us with a bird; it is more than likely, if we are not ornithologists, that we've never seen it, only heard it. Two successive musical notes may have the same association. (But we must insist that the element of association in music is less than in the other two arts, and some might claim that over most music it is not there at all.)

Plainly too there is a sense in which we can 'see' a picture at a glance. But if so we've not *really* seen it. As we look closely we shall be experiencing it over a period of time, and may well say that 'the eye is led from A to B'.

In Figure 2, notice how the thousands of spears are like forces in a magnetic field, how the line of the river leads you to the peaceful distance. But we have been talking about seeing a picture at a glance. The picture is entitled *The Suicide of Saul*. How long was it before you spotted the actual suicide? I am sure you didn't take it in as you first looked at the picture.

In the Rubens in Figure 3, see how the lines of the picture lead you from left to right. Here too I am sure you didn't take in the picture at a glance, but had to allow your eye to follow through.

QUESTION

Notice that all these arts borrow phrases from each other. We may speak of light and shade in a piece of music, of the word-painting of a poem, of the harmony of a painting; we may ask of a painting or a piece of music, 'What does it say to you?' Are these mere metaphors? Or are there really parallels?

Figure 2 Brueghel, The Suicide of Saul (*Kunsthistorisches Museum, Vienna*)

DISCUSSION

I hope you questioned the phrase *'mere* metaphor'. A metaphor is valid only if there are really parallels! In fact metaphorical language may be more true, more real than non-metaphorical. It is worth remembering that we can record sounds visually, and the rhythm of the sounds is reproduced in the rhythm of the visual image.

Figure 3   Rubens, The Allegory of War, *Pitti Palace, Florence (Mansell Collection)*

QUESTION

In the discussion of the second question on p. 26 above there was one word or concept which I used in discussing all three arts. What was it?

ANSWER

Form. This is a very elementary discussion, intended to raise questions rather than to provide answers. The essential points which I want you to bear in mind are that all three arts are different from one another because they operate in different media, and similar to one another because they are drawing on human experience and because there are either direct relationships (time and rhythm in music and literature, images and symbols in literature and painting) or parallels (there is a marvellous story of the philosopher John Locke asking a friend blind from birth what the word *scarlet* conveyed to him, and being answered, 'The sound of a trumpet'); and that in all three arts form is essential to meaning.

You might be interested to think about a work of Dante Gabriel Rossetti (1828–82). Rossetti's father was Italian, and some of his own best literary work lay in translation from the Italian. He was trained as an artist, but was not the sort of student to apply himself with self-discipline, and remained 'notably weak in anatomy, and without any scientific knowledge of perspective'. Still he was primarily a painter, and as such a leading figure in the so-called Pre-Raphaelite

Brotherhood, which aimed to go back beyond Raphael and all that followed him, to treat simple rather than magnificent subjects, to use purity of colour and line in the pursuit of vivid realism.

All through his life he had an astonishing gift for words, and showed himself a poet of rich and exotic language, using words to create visual pictures: colour-language is never far from his pen. He wrote some sonnets for pictures which he himself had painted, and the comparison of picture and poem is of particular interest. I should like you to look at the picture 'Astarte Syriaca' in the Colour Supplement, a study of the great love and fertility goddess of Syria. It is perhaps Rossetti's most overpowering picture, a tribute at once to the power of love, and to William Morris's wife Jane, who was the sitter.

And now read the sonnet that goes with the picture:

Astarte Syriaca
(For a Picture)

Mystery: lo! betwixt the sun and moon .
   Astarte of the Syrians: Venus Queen
   Ere Aphrodite was. In silver sheen
Her twofold girdle clasps the infinite boon
Of bliss whereof the heaven and earth commune:
   And from her neck's inclining flower-stem lean
   Love-freighted lips and absolute eyes that wean
The pulse of hearts to the spheres' dominant tune.

Torch-bearing, her sweet ministers compel
   All thrones of light beyond the sky and sea
   The witnesses of Beauty's face to be:
That face, of Love's all-penetrative spell
Amulet, talisman, and oracle, –
   Betwixt the sun and moon a mystery.

I am not proposing to comment on the way he uses the two artistic media. I'd like you to think about that for yourself.

HISTORY AND PHILOSOPHY (by Arthur Marwick)

John Ferguson, there, chose deliberately to discuss the differences and similarities of only three of the arts, music, art, and literature: he left out history and philosophy.

EXERCISE

Both history and philosophy, in their own different ways, do seem to separate themselves off from these three other arts. Explain this with regard to (a) history, and (b) philosophy.

SPECIMEN ANSWER

(a)   It's difficult to put it neatly in a few words (and you will in a few weeks be coming to my rather full discussion of what history is as well as how it relates to the other arts disciplines). But you might have said something to the effect that history actually happened, whereas art music and literature are deliberately created by individual human beings. Or you might have stressed that history embraces a wide range of human activities, political, economic, social, military, as well as cultural. Music art and literature are very specific activities. Linked to this is the point that the study of history involves the study of a vast range of documents. These, I was going to say, might be considered 'the ingredients' of history, as paint, canvas, and in the other sense, colour and shape or form, are the ingredients of painting, but really (and this is the whole point of this contrast) we are not comparing like with like. You cannot compare art, a particular activity, with particular artefacts, with history, the whole complex of past human experience. What you can compare is the *study* of history, with the study of art and art history: then many of the techniques, and many of the problems are very similar. Actually, as you will learn when you come to Unit 3, when at university we speak of 'history', we do not mean the whole past as it happened, but rather the systematic study of that past, the study of history and the writing of history.The writer of history, obviously, encounters some of the same problems as, say, the writer of a novel, and, certainly, of the writer of a book of literary criticism.

(b)   One cannot say that philosophy has an independent existence in the way that history, in the sense of the past, has. In so far as philosophy consists of the philosophical writings of philosophers, it can perhaps be compared with the three 'creative' arts. However, philosophical writing does not usually aim to appeal to the senses and the emotions in the way that the creative arts, in one way or another, do (however much they may also appeal to the intellectual senses). Philosophy is concerned with the establishment of truths about existence, and with analysing our fundamental concepts, such as those of knowledge, proof, truth, subjectivity, existence.

In that there is a philosophical element in music, art, and literature, and also, indeed, in written history, philosophy overlaps all of the other arts subjects. But as will become apparent when you get to Unit 13, philosophers, seeking always to be rigorous and unambiguous in what they write, have a mode of expression which does separate them from both the writers of literature and the writers of history.

A WORD ON RELIGION (by Arthur Marwick)

After you have had three weeks' study on history, three weeks on literature, three weeks on music, three weeks on philosophy, and three weeks on art and art history, you will have two weeks on religion. The arts, or the humanities, are concerned with human experience and human creative activity. Religion, quite obviously, has been central to human experience down through the ages. Much of our greatest architecture, as well as art and music, have been fundamentally religious in character. As a novel of the Victorian period, *Jane Eyre* is pervaded by the religious attitudes of the time. The question remains: should the study of religion be regarded as a separate independent discipline, or should religion rather be treated as an area of human experience which can be studied through the various other disciplines?

EXERCISE

Which different aspects of religion do you think might properly be studied by the five arts disciplines already mentioned? Take history, philosophy, literature, art history, and music in turn.

SPECIMEN ANSWER

History might study the way religious institutions have developed through time, and their relationships with the rest of society. Philosophy might study religious beliefs, and the truth of religious claims. Literature, obviously, could study the great works of religious literature – the Bible for example. Thus religious art and architecture would be reserved to art history, and religious music to music.

But wouldn't there perhaps be something missing that not all of these disciplines together could get at? That's a question to be left for the moment without an answer. Many questions in arts courses do not have answers. But you will be better able to attempt an answer of your own after reading Units 19 and 20.

4 THE FOURTH AIM OF THE COURSE
(by Arthur Marwick, Ellie Mace and Arnold Kettle)

This aim runs on from Aim 3, reading 'But nevertheless to stress the general idea that the Arts disciplines should not be kept in separate compartments but can and should be brought together both in the study of particular problems and in any comprehensive study of the values and standards of civil society.' First, just a quick word about the phrase 'values and standards of civil society'. 'Values and standards' include social customs and behaviour, political organization, modes of thought and expression, as well as cultural achievements; 'civil society' is just a briefer way of saying 'civilized human society'. What we are saying is that to study anything important, whether it is a specific problem, or problems concerning the whole of society, you will need more than one discipline you will need an interdisciplinary or a multidisciplinary approach.

That was the basic point being made by Television Programme 1: such an important movement as romanticism, affected as it was by the great historical events of the Industrial Revolution and the French Revolution, and involving all the arts, can only be comprehended through a multidisciplinary approach. Similarly, if one were to study the question of the effects of the Industrial Revolution on society and the arts. Thus, in the extended final part of this course, we involve you in a multidisciplinary study of the question 'Arts and Society in the Age of Industrialization'. Equally if you are to discuss such topics as 'Women in Society', 'Censorship' or 'The Impact of the Mass Media' you would need to adopt a multidisciplinary approach.

To round off this Introduction we are now going to look in some detail at another of those particular problems which requires a multidisciplinary approach. Arnold Kettle is going to discuss the question of 'The Artist and Society', a question already raised by W. H. Auden's contribution to the television programme, and as you will see, Auden comes up again immediately.

THE ARTIST AND SOCIETY (by Arnold Kettle)

A Question of Commitment

The question of the relation between the artist and society has arisen in contemporary Europe most often in the form of a discussion about the 'commitment' of the artist. Should the artist be 'committed' to some cause or aim, or should he see himself as 'neutral' (as an artist, if not as a citizen) in the conflicts and arguments of the day? Should art be recognized as having at least an element of propaganda in it, or should the artist avoid taking sides and see his art as something 'above the struggle'? Does art serve a greater, more inclusive end or is it to be thought of, rather, as an end in itself?

The two points of view were expressed in the 1940s by, among many others, the writers Jean-Paul Sartre and W. H. Auden. Here is Sartre in his *What is Literature*?:

> We must take up a position *in our literature*, because literature is in essence a taking of position . . . We will be able to safeguard literature only if we undertake the job of de-mystifying our public. For the same reason the writer's duty is to take sides against all injustices, wherever they may come from.

Contrast this with a passage, written a few years earlier, from Auden's poem on the death of W. B. Yeats:

> For poetry makes nothing happen: it survives
> In the valley of its making where executives
> Would never want to tamper . . . it survives,
> A way of happening, a mouth.

There are of course many variations within the two camps – the 'committed' and the 'pure' – and not all artists see the issue in that way at all. But it is not hard to recognize a real and understandable divergence of view here. The 'committed' artist insists that every work of art necessarily has a certain *effect* on those who see or read or hear it, that the artist therefore, whether he wants to or not, influences people, expresses – as Sartre puts it – a 'position' or attitude or point of view towards society, even if he himself may not be conscious of it. The 'pure' artists puts a different emphasis on his activity. He tends to ignore the possible social effects of his work and to insist that his job is, rather, to express as fully as possible the truth or beauty or significance of whatever it is he feels the need, as an artist of integrity, to express. If he feels some sort of 'commitment' it is to his art or to his integrity as an artist that he will be most likely to refer. He is likely to feel that if he pays too much attention to the direct social effects of his work, his art will probably suffer.

It is a complex and tricky dispute and the more you think about it the more you will realize that attempts to describe it in simple black and white terms are bound to be pretty unsatisfactory. As in most disputes the words the disputants use are not always defined in quite the same way and comparatively few contenders on either side take the more 'extreme' positions. 'Committed' artists do not all agree as to the ways their social responsibilities should be exercised or precisely what 'taking sides' implies. Few 'pure' artists would claim that they had *no* social responsibilities. When W. H. Auden, in expressing the thought that poetry is self-sufficient and 'makes nothing happen', uses an image which suggests that poetry is a 'mouth' he is presumably thinking of a mouth as something through which the artist expresses himself, his personal 'voice'. A voice which cries out irrespective of who happens to be listening. But of course when the poetic artist, like the prophets of old, uses his mouth he does not merely express himself, he also communicates, and this *may* make something happen and Auden would of course admit this. So one must beware of oversimplifying the question. Yet you will probably agree that there is a real, and not just imaginary, problem here and that people concerned with the arts will tend to veer in one direction or the other – towards an emphasis on the artist's responsibilities to society or towards an emphasis on the 'pure' or autonomous nature of art which reaches an extreme expression in the phrase 'art for art's sake'.

EXERCISE

This is for your own benefit, simply to help you clarify your mind on these issues. No need to make heavy weather of it.

1   Give three arguments which seem to you to constitute a strong case in favour of the 'committed' artist.
2   Give three reasons which seem to you powerful arguments *against* the view of the role of the artist put forward by Sartre.

DISCUSSION

There are bound to be divergencies in students' answers to these questions, for the field of argument is a spacious one.

1   Among the strongest arguments for 'commitment' you may have found:
(a)   that the artist cannot claim exemption from the normal social responsibility to make sure that the effects of his actions are not harmful to others;
(b)   that the artist, because he is more articulate than others has a *special* responsibility to use his gifts on behalf of human good;

(c)   that since everyone's actions affect others it is better to be conscious rather than unconscious of those effects;

(d)   that art itself suffers if artists do not recognize their moral responsibilities;

(e)   that art is created for people rather than for the personal satisfaction of the artist;

(f)   that 'art for art's sake' is a meaningless phrase denying any sort of objective criteria for judging art;

(g)   that neutrality in practice tends to mean helping the stronger side;

(h)   that great artists have in fact been deeply committed to the service of humanity and often to specific contemporary courses;

(i)   that no activity can ever be isolated as 'an end in itself'.

2   Among the dangers of 'commitment' are:

(a)   the danger of making up your mind without considering all the facts and issues (i.e. prejudging a situation and underestimating its complexity);

(b)   the danger of allowing one's personal judgement to be overruled by the immediate pressures of some authority or government or common opinion;

(c)   the danger that the artist may feel that he has some special right to know what is good for other people;

(d)   the danger of falsifying facts because to do so may seem to help one's 'cause' or 'position';

(e)   that the artist may stray from the aesthetic province, where he has competence, and trespass in areas where he has no special gifts;

(f)   that as art is not 'useful' in the sense that a pamphlet or recipe or book of rules may be, to judge art by its practical utility is irrelevant and can easily reduce its real value;

(g)   that the effects of art are long-term; artists have often been 'in advance of their time' (i.e. condemned by the orthodox social values of their day but later hailed as more perceptive than their critics);

(h)   assuming that the value of art lies in its moral effects;

(i)   that as the 'committed' artist has made up his mind about the question he is dealing with before he actually grapples with it, he therefore leaves himself no room for discovery.

I am not suggesting that all these arguments are equally strong, nor that they are the only possible arguments. But they may help you to see the sort of issues people feel are at stake when they argue about the 'commitment of the artist'.

This question of 'commitment' is, however, only one aspect or example of the problem we are concerned with. Our object is to consider in a more general way the relationship between the artist and society and we shall do this by taking a look at some examples of this relationship at different stages of social development. We shall find, inevitably, that the question of the position of the artist in different societies cannot be completely isolated from a consideration of the general social relationships of those societies. Thus, though we shall try to concentrate on art and the artist (the poet in particular), we shall find ourselves involved to some extent in more general social and historical problems.

STUDY NOTE 3: THE PURPOSE OF NOTE-TAKING
(by Ellie Mace)

Earlier on I tried to explain why we include exercises in the text, and why it is important for you to take the time to think out your own ideas. If you write down answers to exercises and questions and make a note of any ideas that occur to you as you go along certain other benefits also accrue:

1   *you have a written record of some of your ideas*, and
2   *in your own words*

1   On p. 18 I asked you to make some notes on Auden's comments in the TV programme and to keep them by you. You'll have noticed that Arnold Kettle has taken up and enlarged on Auden's theme (i.e. 'A question of commitment') and

given you a different point of view on it. He then asked you to think of three arguments for and against the 'committed' artist. Now that both sides of the argument have been presented and you've had a little more time to think about it, are your arguments against the 'committed' artist any different from those you jotted down earlier? Have your ideas or has your point of view changed at all? If so how, and why? What *now* do you think are the main issues? Just look over the notes you made earlier on and think about these questions for a moment.

I imagine that you may be feeling rather overwhelmed by the whole question – that you can't really decide one way or the other because there seem to be some good arguments on both sides. Perhaps you feel you need some of these points spelled out and a lot more time to think about them. By contrast when you were asked earlier if you agreed with Auden's point of view you may have been able to give a positive answer one way or the other. So what progress have you made you might wonder? Well the answer is that you *have* made solid progress. You have understood enough to recognize that this is not the sort of question that can be answered very easily. You have begun to think hard about some of the issues involved and have seen that you need to understand a great deal more about others before you can reach any satisfactory conclusions of your own. Your mind is 'opening up' to all the possibilities and consequently you are bound to feel confused – as first you consider one side of the argument, then the other, and then back again. If you had some weeks to consider the subject and produce an essay on it you would no doubt still feel fairly confused and ill-prepared. The point is that when we effectively say, 'Stop. Write', we are simply asking you to show how far you have got in your deliberations. We are not expecting you to have come up with the 'answer' or to have 'solved' the problem. (Neither do we suppose that you will never think about the subject again.) What we expect is more along the lines of a progress report. And this brings me back to the notes you make as you work through the units. These form your own private progress report. When you look back over work you've done in the past, often quite recently, you may be amazed to see how far you've come. (Perhaps this is even true of your thoughts about Auden and the 'question of commitment' so far.) So when the crunch comes and, however muddled you feel, you have to get your thoughts on to paper, it's a good idea to look back over your jottings. When you see how much thought you *have* put in and to what extent your understanding is enlarged you should feel much more confident that what you have to say is worth saying. And that should enable you to *write* with some degree of confidence.

The other advantage of a written record is that it is permanent. You can return to your notes at any time and particularly when you come to revise the course.

2   A major point in favour of jotting down notes is that they are *your* notes; they represent what you understand of the text, reflect what interests you, and because they are expressed in your words they become as much your ideas as the unit author's (indeed they may not be his/hers ar all.) Also, if you are in the habit of making your own notes you are far less likely to be guilty of plagiarism when, for example in a TMA, you are asked to present arguments given by unit or set book authors. Then, unless you quite deliberately try to write your own (condensed) version of what an author is saying, it's sometimes tempting just to reproduce what he has said more or less word for word. It's actually quite difficult to avoid doing so when you are directed to a shortish section of the text which must be summarized as part of your answer. Under these circumstances the only ways to avoid plagiarism are:
(a)   Either jot down notes on the section and re-write them using your own words as far as possible – be selective and only include the main points,
(b)   or acknowledge your source – that is, quote or paraphrase the author making it clear that you are doing so. (I shall say more about quotation in Study Note 5).

In fact it would be extremely unlikely that the bulk of an essay would involve simply reproducing other people's arguments. If you find yourself doing so for more than about a page you should wonder whether you've understood the question you've been asked. (In the 'essay' on abortion you were asked to summarize two opposing points of view in order to examine the implications of holding either view – and this examination should have formed the main part of your answer.) However, it is essential for any student to be able to make brief but clear notes of an author's argument or of the contents of an important chapter in a book. I will return to the subject of note-taking in Study Note 6.

THE ARTIST AND SOCIETY (by Arnold Kettle) CONTINUED

Art, in the general sense of describing a form of human activity, is a rather modern concept. It is really only within the last two hundred years that people have talked much about 'art' as such and the image we tend to have of the 'artist' as a lonely genius, eccentric 'odd man out', bohemian rebel (you know what is meant when someone – who doesn't generally much care for art – says to you, 'Oh yes, so-and-so's boy is very artistic') – and this view doesn't go back much beyond the nineteenth century. So we should beware of letting this sort of association colour too much our view of the subject.

Artists (i.e. the people who composed songs and poems, made masks, led the dances, beat the drums) in primitive societies[†] were certainly not thought of as eccentrics, though we know they were honoured for their skills. But primitive art is mostly, in the nature of things, anonymous. If a man in a tribal society achieves a reputation as a poet neither he nor his audience finds it easy to distinguish precisely what *he* had added to the store of traditional poetry which he works on and transmits. He no doubt adds something: that is what being a poet or minstrel involves. But he works on material (the history, myths and experience of the tribe) which is not peculiarly 'his' and his own contribution – the new ways he finds of telling a story or describing an incident – itself becomes absorbed into the material and within a few generations could not be identified as 'his'. Whereas the modern poet composes and publishes his poetry in relative isolation and, except for 'revisions' which can never wholly obliterate the 'original', leaves it alone; the poet in earlier societies worked in different ways and had inevitably a different attitude to his art. Art and 'craft' or 'skill' were in fact much closer to one another. A twentieth-century philosopher writing about art can make the distinction between 'art' and 'craft' the very core of his definition of art:

> Most people who write about art today seem to think that it is some kind of craft; and this is the main error against which a modern aesthetic theory must fight.[*]

This is not conceivable in a more primitive society. The city librarian of a modern town may catalogue his books under the headings 'Fine Arts' (painting, literature, music, etc.) and 'Useful Arts' (cooking, handicraft, etc.) but he will find it hard to decide whether architecture, for instance, is 'fine' or 'useful' and to men and women in their earlier stages of development the distinction simply did not exist. It is worth asking why the distinction came about and how far it is valid.

[†]Note that the word 'primitive' as used here does not imply any value-judgement, or any sort of contempt. 'Primitive' societies are, as such, neither better nor worse than 'advanced' or 'developed' ones. They are simpler (less complex) and historically come earlier. That is all.

[*]R. G. Collingwood, *The Principles of Art* (1938), p. 26.

Figure 4   Fine or useful?   (By kind permission of the Hon. Robert Erskine)

EXERCISE

Architecture is both a fine art (buildings can be beautiful) and a useful one (obviously). How do you see the relation between the two? Write down (a) three examples of beautiful buildings and (b) three utilitarian considerations an architect has to bear in mind when designing a house. Then try to decide whether the two aspects are connected in any way.

DISCUSSION

This is a big question and we can't hope to answer it fully.

(a)   Your three beautiful buildings may have been obviously functional (a railway station or power station, a bridge) and you may come to the conclusion that the reason we consider them beautiful is because they do their job so well and economically. But the issues are complicated. A building can be very servicable, a house very comfortable and 'well-designed' without necessarily striking us as beautiful. Twentieth-century building tends to emphasize 'function' but it is hard to say where 'function' stops. May it not be part of the 'function' of a house to delight the eye? And if we describe a building as 'fussy' is it the shape, pure and simple, or something to do with its function that we are thinking of? When we admire the proportions of a Queen Anne house aren't we including in our admiration such qualities as 'airiness' as well as harmonious dimensions? On the other hand does our admiration of a fine cathedral have much to do with its utility? We do not think it less beautiful because (a) the architect has omitted to provide a lavatory or (b) we may not believe in God. Yet if we say that its beauty has nothing to do with some quality of human aspiration expressed in its proportions and its thrust, we are almost certainly deceiving ourselves.

(b)   You may have written down such considerations as plenty of window-space, adequate sanitation and provision against land-subsidence. At first glance these seem to have little or nothing to do with aesthetic considerations. Yet it is hard to imagine a beautiful house without windows and (despite the Tower of Pisa and Chesterfield Church spire) we do not normally admire a building that is on the skew.

Figure 5   The Leaning Tower of Pisa   (Photo: Camera Press, London)

The object of this question was not to extract 'right' answers but merely to set you thinking about a subject which is more complex than people sometimes imagine.

The Art of Aristocratic Society

In the middle of the sixteenth century there began to be written, in English, poems which, despite differences in language and spelling, are unmistakably more 'modern' in tone than the literature of the Middle Ages. Sir Thomas Wyatt's poems were not printed in his lifetime (though some were shortly after his death in 1542) but were circulated in manuscript among his friends, aristocrats or near-aristocrats of the Court circle in the time of King Henry VIII. Here is one of them (the spelling has been modernized).

> Forget not yet the tried intent
> Of such a truth as I have meant,
> My great travail so gladly spent
>   Forget not yet.
>
> Forget not yet when first began
> The weary life you know since when,
> The suit, the service none tell can.
>   Forget not yet.

> Forget not yet the great assays,
> The cruel wrong, the scornful ways,
> The painful patience in denies,
>   Forget not yet.
>
> Forget not yet, forget not this,
> How long ago hath been and is
> The mind that never meant amiss,
>   Forget not yet.
>
> Forget not then thine own approved,
> The which so long hath thee so loved,
> Whose steadfast faith yet never moved,
>   Forget not this.

We had better start by making sure the poem has been understood, though without, at this point, going into any sort of detailed discussion about the way to read a poem (this will come in Units 6–8). It is, however, important to remember that almost all poems have to be read many times before their full force is felt. It is not enough to read it through once or twice and have a vague idea of what it is 'about'. A poem like this is a compressed and highly-wrought expression of a complex and intense emotion. Unless you have shared to some extent the poet's feelings you have not really read the poem.

EXERCISE

Let us take a few important points of meaning:

1   What exactly does 'tried intent' imply?

2   Are you sure you understand the meaning of the words 'travail', 'suit', 'service', 'assays'? Does any connecting link strike you as drawing these words together?

Jot your answers down in your notebook, then compare your thoughts with mine on the next page.

Figure 6
Holbein's portrait of Sir Thomas Wyatt
(Royal Collection; copyright reserved)

DISCUSSION

1   Neither word is really difficult yet their juxtaposition involves a particular effect. 'Intent' as a noun means simply 'intention', but its more common use as an adverb in such a phrase as 'to be intent upon' gives it a special force, suggesting a certain *intensity* in the action and, indeed, reminding us that an intention scarcely exists except as an action. A 'tried intent' is an intention *tested* (by time or experience) and therefore must have involved 'doing' as well as 'intending to do'. So the whole phrase suggests not some vague intention or feeling but a series of actions, tasks or tests which embody and give proof of the speaker's truth or fidelity.

2   'Travail' means work or labour (reminding us of the Norman French formerly spoken by the British aristocracy) and 'assays' again is from the French 'essayer' – to try. 'Suit'* and 'service' are both words linked very strongly with the social obligations entered into by people in feudal society. A tenant brought his 'suit' to his feudal lord and rendered 'service' to him. These services might involve payment of money but would more likely mean the obligation to give so many days' work or produce or military service.

The points worth noticing are that all these words are (a) the common coin of the feudal system of relationships in which the tenant or suitor performs certain tasks in exchange for the goodwill of the lord or master, (b) they all imply (like 'tried intent') actions, not merely ideas.

And yet – you will probably be feeling – isn't it a bit odd to be making this sort of emphasis about the poem when it is, after all, clearly a love poem, a poem expressing the private, personal emotions of a lover addressing his mistress?

Yes, it *is* a love poem, expressing a personal emotion of a particular kind, the feeling of a man about his lover. It represents a private sort of art which could only arise in a society where at least some people had the means and leisure to develop a relatively private life.

Although it is a private poem, the publishing of it is a social act. But the audience with whom the poet shares his emotions is a *limited* audience, a specific bit of society, rather than the society as a whole. It is an aristocratic poem, not only in the sense that its original readers were likely to be ladies and gentlemen, but that the very nature of the situation involved could only arise among the leisured class of a more or less aristocratic society. The love-situation of the poem – the man presenting his suit to the lady who keeps him dangling while she makes up her mind – could only occur *in the form it does* in a society at a particular stage of development.

We have noticed how the language of the poem is the language of a particular sort of social set-up, a feudal social order in which the relationships between each person in society are defined in some sort of contract. Try reading the poem through, ignoring for the moment your knowledge that it is a love poem, written to the poet's mistress. You will find, I think, that the poem makes perfectly good sense as the expression of the feelings of a courtier who has fallen foul of the king or indeed of any lesser feudal gentleman who has had trouble with his 'lord'. The very word 'mistress', incidentally, is an interesting one. Except in a feudal society it is hard to imagine the words 'lover' and 'mistress' being interchangeable. If we still use the word today it is as a historical hangover, for few people today really feel like describing a lover as a mistress. In other words the very nature of the poet's art is affected by the nature and language of the society within which he is operating, despite the fact that he is expressing emotions of the most personal and even private kind.

How do you explain the fact that what is pretty clearly a love poem can also be read as a poem addressed by a feudal vassal to his lord?

---

*'Suit' is short for 'suit of court' which meant originally attendance by a tenant at the court of his lord. It came to mean a petition. This poem is a sort of petition for redress of grievances.

The explanation is partially or superficially linguistic, i.e. the same words come to have different meanings or functions. E.g. 'thine own *approved*' can be a lover or a favoured applicant, just as a mistress can mean the woman you go to bed with or your female boss (or the head of a ladies' college). But to leave it at that is merely to transfer the problem slightly, for the question remains: how does it happen that the same word comes to have different meanings?

The explanation is that in life there can seldom if ever be a total separation between private and public. Even people who lead 'secret' lives generally find that it is themselves rather than others whom they most deceive. When we speak of 'feudal relationships' we normally think of the more public aspects of such relationships – relationships involving the payment of goods or 'services' in the economic or military sense. But the essence of the word 'service' is that it puts someone in an inferior relationship to someone else (the modern phrase 'social service' tries to obliterate this but does not wholly succeed). This worked in feudal society on both the public and private planes. The rules of courtship among the upper classes were determined by the general rules of social behaviour, just as the very idea of a marriage 'contract' can only exist in a society in which, in general, relationships are thought of in terms of 'contract'. This was partly because aristocratic marriages always in practice involved property deals. And the higher you went up in the social scale the less could the private and public realms be separated. *Naturally* (a word worth pausing over) the king's marriage was a public affair, and the terms of the contract would have the force and form of a treaty between states. And equally naturally the relationship between Wyatt and his lover was the relationship of people living *and feeling* within the bounds of a feudal society. People can only feel what they dare to feel. Love is a changing concept involving changing feelings and no more exempt from the influences of the outside world than anything else. Wyatt is kicking against the pricks of the courtly conventions of aristocratic love-making. But to have escaped them he would have had to escape the social class in which he lived, scarcely a practical possibility for an up-and-coming young English gentleman of the early sixteenth century.

The artist in feudal society tends to be either (a) a gentleman (like Wyatt) who produces art in his spare time, as an accomplishment which adds something to the quality of the life he leads, or (b) someone dependent on the patronage of a member of the ruling class. This does not necessarily mean that he is 'committed' to an aristocratic society in the sense of feeling impelled to defend it. His art may, indeed, contain, explicitly or implicitly, very deep criticism of that society (e.g. in the eighteenth century, Fielding, Mozart); but the criticism is made in the language and largely within the framework of an aristocratic set-up.

QUESTION

In what ways would you say Wyatt's poem expresses an acceptance of the values of the aristocracy of his time, in what ways a criticism of those values?

DISCUSSION

To the extent that Wyatt uses the language and concepts of the feudal social order it is fair to say that in some sense he 'accepts' that society. As we have seen, this poem is written in terms which involve a particular view of the relationship between the sexes. The lover, whose emotions form the content of the poem, seems to accept a particular role – the role of suitor, who through the performance of various services and the consequent proofs of his fidelity, offers himself to the lady, who in turn acts a particular rôle, that of mistress, more or less arbitrarily accepting or rejecting the proofs of loyalty offered. To the extent that Wyatt's poem is a product and expression of this situation, it may be said that he is operating as an artist within the accepted terms and conventions of his society. And this is, indeed, a poem written within a common convention of the time – a lover's complaint. Almost all poets of the sixteenth century, including Shakespeare, wrote this sort of poem.

Yet in another sense it does not seem satisfactory to describe Wyatt's poem as one of acceptance of the values of the aristocracy of his time. For the deepest emotion that the poem expresses is resentment. The lover's 'truth' is contrasted, time after time, with the lady's cruelty. The power she exercises is a power abused. It would not be false to say that this is a poem about power: social and sexual power are linked in it in half a dozen intricate but obvious ways. So that imperceptibly the lover's complaint becomes a complaint about the way power operates in Wyatt's society. That is why the 'conventional' images of the rejected lover upon which the poem is built are so effective. In particular the reiterated words 'Forget not yet' come to have the force of a protest: 'Forget not this'.

So it seems to me that the poem is both a product of and a criticism of Wyatt's society and expresses the ambiguous and contradictory nature of his relationship to that society.

STUDY NOTE 4: SOME EXERCISES (by Ellie Mace)

Again, several exercises were included in this section of the text. I hope you had a go at some of them at least. The exercise on p. 36 is an example of a question to which there is no one correct answer (and so is representative of many of the questions you will be asked in this course). As Arnold Kettle says, the object of it is to 'set you thinking'. So you shouldn't be upset if you thought rather differently or, indeed, not at all, as long as you can now see the point of the question and understand the discussion of it. Similarly I don't think you should worry if you couldn't guess the meaning of the words in Wyatt's poem (exercise on p. 38.) I think Arnold Kettle set this exercise in order to underline the importance of reading poetry with care, and making sure that you do understand the meaning of the words. In such cases as this you should obviously pay close attention to the discussions of the exercises.

But I hope that you were able to come up with some thoughts about the question on p. 40, because this question touches directly on the theme of this part of the unit. Consequently it is a 'key' exercise. Arnold Kettle actually expresses his intentions quite clearly on p. 33. Did you note the relevant sentence? It is:

> Our object is to consider in a more general way the relationship between the artist and society and we shall do this by taking a look at some examples of this relationship at differing stages of social development.

Wyatt's poem, and his society, is the first instance he selects for study. I point this out because when you are working through a unit it's quite easy to get 'bogged down' in the detail at times, and to lose sight of the main line of argument or the theme of the unit. If you find this happening a good tip is simply to write out the theme(s) of the unit in block letters and keep them propped up in front of you as you work. You can then remind yourself of the general direction the argument is taking whenever you feel you don't really see the point of a particular section of the text.

THE ARTIST AND SOCIETY (by Arnold Kettle) CONTINUED

Blake's London

The next poem I want you to read can scarcely be called 'aristocratic'. It is by William Blake (1757–1827) and was written in the 1790s – the time, you'll recall, of both the French and Industrial Revolutions – and included among Blake's *Songs of Experience*, published in 1793.

Figure 7   Blake's own illustration of his poem in the Songs of Experience *(Syndics of the Fitzwilliam Museum, Cambridge)*

London

> I wander thro' each charter'd street
> Near where the charter'd Thames does flow,
> And mark in every face I meet
> Marks of weakness, marks of woe.
>
> In every cry of every Man,
> In every Infant's cry of fear,
> In every voice, in every ban,
> The mind-forg'd manacles I hear.
>
> How the Chimney-sweeper's cry
> Every black'ning Church appals;
> And the hapless Soldier's sigh
> Runs in blood down Palace walls.
>
> But most thro' midnight streets I hear
> How the youthful Harlot's curse
> Blasts the new born Infant's tear,
> And blights with plagues the Marriage hearse.

Read the poem through several times, until you are sure you understand it, at least in its general meaning.

Then jot down answers to the following questions:

1   What does the word 'charter'd' in the first stanza mean?
2   What does the phrase 'the mind-forg'd manacles' mean?

These are questions involving understanding of the primary meaning of the words of the poem – as opposed to later questions which involve the more general meaning or interpretation of the poem, so we had better deal with them first. Try to find the answers yourself but then look them up before going any further.

DISCUSSION

1 'Charter'd' means authorized or let out by royal charter, i.e. the old chartered companies of the City of London (goldsmiths, merchant tailors, etc.). The word emphasizes the *commercial* nature of the city, even the river is seen as *property*. (N.B. It is interesting that in the first draft of the poem Blake used the word 'dirty' and later changed it to 'chartered'. Dirty is more immediately vivid but the word 'chartered' makes the reader think more and deepens the *analytical* nature of the poem. Blake is not merely describing what London looks like; he is probing more deeply into the nature of the city and the implications of its dirtiness.)

2 'Mind-forg'd manacles' means chains forged by the human mind. It is part of the burden of this poem that *ideas* as well as physical constraints can imprison people. If you found this a difficult phrase to understand it is because the thought behind it (rather than the actual words) may be unfamiliar. But looking the words up in a dictionary (which could have helped with 'chartered') will not have been of much help. This phrase has the kind of difficulty one must puzzle out for oneself, and, in an important sense, the object of the poem is to force the reader to puzzle it out. Once you have got a sense of the overall meaning of the poem as a whole the phrase 'mind-forg'd manacles' itself falls into place: you realize that what Blake is referring to is the power of the human mind to produce and impose ideas which act as chains, perpetuating fear and weakness and woe.

EXERCISE

Now try to answer these rather more complex questions about the poem.

1 What do you understand by the lines:

> How the Chimney-sweeper's cry
> Every black'ning Church appals?

2 How can a sigh run in blood down a wall?
3 What seems to you to be the point of the final image of the poem: the 'marriage hearse'?

Think seriously about each question in turn and jot down a sentence indicating how you would answer them in a discussion of the poem. Then compare your notes with the specimen answers, which are to be taken as suggestive possibilities, *not* the only possible answer.

DISCUSSION

1 Worth remembering (if you haven't) is that the chimney sweep of 1793 was a boy who actually climbed up inside the chimney, which, besides being unpleasant and dangerous, also undermined health because of the effect of the soot on lungs, etc. The chimney sweeper's cry has already been evoked in more general terms in the previous stanza, it is therefore both particular (one child crying out) and general (for *every* man and *every* child are shown crying in fear).

The chimney sweeper and the Church may seem at first to be separate: in fact they are linked by (a) the soot from the chimney that blackens the church. 'Blacken' has a moral as well as visual force. The church is blackened not only by the soot but by its failure to deal with the cry of the chimney sweeper, which is the cry of the agonized and impoverished of a whole society; (b) the chimney and the Church (which probably has a spire) are juxtaposed, rising together as part of the landscape of Blake's England.

This image in fact makes the reader see the Church not as a single building but as part of the complex of commercial England; and the Church is appalled, i.e. horrified, perplexed, faced with a challenge which (it is hinted) it is afraid to meet, perhaps because it is itself blackened, i.e. a part of the industrial set-up.

2   This is an example of a highly condensed poetic image which operates through a complex web of associations. The 'hapless soldier' (like the chimney sweep) is immediately associated by the reader with the faces marked by weakness and woe which dominate Blake's view of London. He is one of many, and his sigh is a part of the general cry of pain and misery which arises from the city. Obviously a sigh cannot quite literally 'run in blood', but the association of the soldier's sigh with blood and of the two with the palace, the centre of authority in the state, are perfectly lucid. And, though the image operates on a deeper level than the purely visual, it has also great visual power. Just as the chimney and the Church are visually connected in the urban landscape, so here we get a strong visual image of a palace wall not merely smeared with the blood of dead soldiers but bloody with atrocities that still go on.

3   A marriage and a funeral are normally seen as opposites – the one of joy and hope, the other of grief and ending. Here they are brought together in an extraordinarily powerful image. The wedding coach becomes a funeral hearse. The institution of marriage, Blake is saying, is corrupted and poisoned by the institution of prostitution. The 'harlot's curse', rising from the chartered streets, blights all human relationships. Blake is referring not only to actual plagues like venereal disease but to the whole phenomenon of 'chartered' or commercialized sex. As he puts it in another poem:

> The Whore & Gambler, by the State
> Licenc'd, build that Nation's Fate.
> The Harlot's cry from Street to Street
> Shall weave Old England's winding Sheet.
> The Winner's shout, the Loser's Curse
> Dance before dead England's Hearse.

I think the main point to notice is that Blake is not merely condemning prostitution in the abstract as a Bad Thing. He is specifically linking it in his language and imagery with the morality of a commercial society and he is condemning in his poem not the harlot (any more than the soldier or the chimney sweep) but the chartered streets and mind-forged manacles which he presents through his art as the essence of London with its all-pervading human misery.

How are we to describe William Blake's relationship, as an artist, to the society he lived in and so deeply criticized, even to the point of rejecting the major social and moral values of the 'Establishment' of his day? Blake, like Wyatt, lived in a class-divided society in which power was in the hands of an aristocracy. But Blake, unlike Wyatt, did not accept in a fundamental sense the necessity of this sort of society. On the contrary, Blake was a revolutionary artist. Pretty obviously the contrast between the two poets cannot be seen in purely individual terms. Blake lived in a revolutionary age: Wyatt did not. Blake found himself in the midst of the flood of democratic ideas and aspirations released by the French Revolution. Wyatt was in the nature of things concerned rather with the operation of more arbitrary tyrannies within the royal court itself. So that when we speak of Wyatt's art as aristocratic, Blake's as revolutionary, we are making statements which only make sense within a whole context of historical development.

Notice, however, that the contrast I am making between Wyatt's and Blake's art is not a question of *subject-matter*. It is not because *Forget not yet* is a love poem that Wyatt's art is not revolutionary. Nor is it because *London* is about a city that Blake's is a revolutionary poem. *London* is every bit as *personal* a poem as *Forget not yet*, Blake's personal emotions are just as much involved as Wyatt's; he begins with 'I' and the strength of his feelings emerges in the incomparable intensity of the whole poem. Indeed it could be argued that Wyatt's poem is the more impersonal, for it has the structure and feeling of one of the conventional 'lover's complaints' of the time. Yet we have seen that Wyatt's too, is not an uncritical poem: in a way it is a complaint against 'mind-forg'd manacles' – the whole feudal conception of the way a man and a woman should behave to one another. So the contrast I am making between the two poems has to be expressed very carefully. What it amounts to is that in an aristocratic society, in which class divisions persist, artists will tend either (like Wyatt) to operate *within* the framework and assumptions of those divisions and therefore to produce art which, however critical in some of its implications, can properly be called aristocratic art; or else (like Blake) to develop their criticisms of society to a point at which they take up a standpoint which cannot be contained within the existing social order: in other words they become revolutionary.

What Wyatt and Blake still have in common, as far as their relationship to their societies is concerned, is that both assume, though from different standpoints, that the poet is a social being who can only live and express himself within a social context or framework. Wyatt accepts, though painfully and – as we have seen – resentfully, the 'rules' of an aristocratic society. He operates as an artist within the approved bounds of that society, writing from the point of view of a member of the Establishment, an aristocratic lover who is hurt and frustrated by the way the love-game of courtly relationships works and impinges on his needs and hopes. Blake, two hundred and fifty years later, born in to a society with a basically similar class *structure* but immensely different in *content*, takes a different 'position' (to use Sartre's phrase). He is a committed revolutionary who sees London as a disgusting human phenomenon embodying relationships and values which he cannot accept. Yet Blake, though he rejects the values of eighteenth-century London, accepts the fact that he is a part of it, just as Wyatt accepts that he is a part of the Tudor court. It does not occur to either artist to try to take himself outside society altogether. The one is a sensitive aristocrat, the other a passionate democrat: the tone of their poetry is, obviously, very different. But both assume that the individual lives and functions within society. Blake makes a further assumption, and one that many sensitive people of his time were making: that it is possible, and indeed necessary, to change society and build a different one embodying different values. He expresses this conviction, you will almost certainly recall, in the best-known of all his poems:

> I will not cease from Mental Fight
> Nor shall my Sword rest in my hand
> Till we have built Jerusalem
> In England's green & pleasant Land.

London must be rebuilt, he is saying, as the new Jerusalem.

An Artist in Victorian Society

Matthew Arnold's *Dover Beach* was first published in 1867, though it had been written in 1852. It is very much a product of nineteenth-century England, and indeed of nineteenth-century Europe; and just as it is impossible to dissociate Blake's *London* from the French Revolution and the Industrial Revolution, one cannot read *Dover Beach* without an awareness of the tensions of mid-Victorian England or of what was going on across the Straits of Dover, the social and intellectual ferment arising out of the revolutions of the vital year 1848.

Dover Beach

The sea is calm tonight.
The tide is full, the moon lies fair
Upon the straits; on the French coast the light
Gleams and is gone; the cliffs of England stand,
Glimmering and vast, out in the tranquil bay.
Come to the window, sweet is the night-air!
Only, from the long line of spray
Where the sea meets the moon-blanched land,
Listen! you hear the grating roar
Of pebbles which the waves draw back, and fling,
At their return, up the high strand,
Begin, and cease, and then again begin,
With tremulous cadence slow, and bring
The eternal note of sadness in.

Figure 8   Dover Beach (Mansell Collection)

Sophocles long ago
Heard it on the Aegean, and it brought
Into his mind the turbid ebb and flow
Of human misery; we
Find also in the sound a thought,
Hearing it by this distant northern sea.

The Sea of Faith
Was once, too, at the full, and round earth's shore
Lay like the folds of a bright girdle furled.
But now I only hear
Its melancholy, long, withdrawing roar,
Retreating, to the breath
Of the night-wind, down the vast edges drear
And naked shingles of the world.

Ah, love, let us be true
To one another! for the world, which seems
To lie before us like a land of dreams,
So various, so beautiful, so new,
Hath really neither joy, nor love, nor light,
Nor certitude, nor peace, nor help for pain;
And we are here as on a darkling plain
Swept with confused alarms of struggle and flight.
Where ignorant armies clash by night.

First, let us try to define as clearly as possible what the poem is doing, before attempting to sum up what it is 'about'.

QUESTION

Say as accurately as you can what is conveyed in the first fourteen lines of the poem.

DISCUSSION

Your answer should have included such points as:

1   The evocation of calm in the opening lines (the important words 'calm', 'fair', 'tranquil', 'sweet') gradually broken or modified (with the word 'only') by the 'eternal note of sadness' brought in by the insistent grating roar of the moving pebbles, drawn down and flung up by the sea. (Note the contrast between the pure moonlight with its effect of motionless serenity and the 'tremulous' movement of the sea.)

2   The poet (with his wife or lover close) stands at the edge of England, whose cliffs – 'glimmering and vast' – face the straits across which the French lighthouse 'gleams and is gone'. There is a special sort of significance about *this* beach and the cliffs which seem to suggest security and protection as though they were guarding England.

QUESTION

What precisely do we learn about 'the eternal note of sadness' in the following lines? (15–28).

DISCUSSION

(a)   Through the references to Sophocles, who wrote tragedies, and the Aegean, a recurring process is suggested, the England of the 1850s linked with the past. The note of sadness is now defined more fully as being associated with a *general phenomenon* 'the turbid ebb and flow of human misery', the movement of the sea compared with the movement of human history. But the sound the poet hears, though it links him and England with the past, has its own special significance (notice how the phrase 'distant northern sea' besides marking a contrast – which suggests perhaps the classical contrast between Mediterranean civilization and northern barbarism – also links England with the world as a whole).

(b)   The special significance of the note of sadness to the poet is now revealed and developed through the complex metaphor of the 'Age of Faith' which is compared to a sea holding together (like a girdle) and offering security to the earth's shores. This phrase 'the Sea of Faith' presumably refers primarily to religious faith, in the mid-nineteenth century being eroded by more sceptical and scientific ideas; but the image also suggests a general sense of *security*. The words 'withdrawing' and 'retreating', reinforced by 'melancholy', 'drear' and 'naked' give a sense of frightening insecurity. Note how the cliffs, once 'glimmering a vast', now have 'vast edges drear'. The personal melancholy of the poet is associated in numerous ways with the insecurity of a whole civilization. We can have no doubt that this poem is referring continuously to the condition – especially the spiritual condition – of England, once secure, now uncertain.

EXERCISE

What do you make of the ending of the poem (lines 29–37)?

DISCUSSION

(a)   Note the sudden movement from contemplation of the outside world (the moonlight, the sea, the roar, the Greeks, the retreat of faith) to the expression of an intimately personal emotion. The switch is so sudden as to suggest almost a sense of panic, for there has not previously been any suggestion (in the 'come to the window' passage) that the lovers might *not* be true to one another.

(b)   The final, long-drawn-out image of the world – what it *seemed* and what it now is felt by the poet to be – is one of almost hopeless disillusionment. Joy, love, light, certitude, peace, comfort are all dismissed as illusions. In their place we are given a cheerless image of lost travellers stranded on a 'darkling' plain 'swept with confused alarms of struggle and flight'. The world has become a place where 'ignorant armies', blinded by and perhaps made invisible by darkness, clash – and the clash is unresolved. Darkness and insecurity and danger have totally replaced the sense of light, calm and confidence of the opening lines of the poem. Dover beach has become an image exciting a sense of fear and dread.

QUESTION

What would you say the poem is essentially about?

DISCUSSION

Obviously there will be different ways of putting it, and different emphases. But most careful readers will probably agree that it is a poem expressing the growing sense of ominous insecurity felt by a cultured middle-class Englishman in the middle of the nineteenth century. It is a moving poem because of the quality of sincerity which the central images convey – a sense of melancholy but honest dread. And it is impressive too because the personal emotions of the poet (or of the character whose feelings are being expressed) are so fully and successfully integrated (through the Dover setting) with the expression of a more public situation – the end of English isolation from the turbulent developments on the continent of Europe. Matthew Arnold is afraid – afraid of those 'ignorant' armies and forces (someone taking an opposite position might call them the forces of democracy) gathering and upsetting the secure serenity of the England which the cliffs of Dover have guarded. And, significantly, at this moment of ominous fear, he turns away from the sound he dreads, from the cliffs, from any kind of public action, to his wife.

> Ah, love, let us be true
> To one another!

That is all there is left. The individual turns from the public world to a private one.

One cannot, of course, draw many generalized conclusions from a single example and I am not wishing to suggest to you that Matthew Arnold's situation was representative of that of all the artists of the Victorian era. Clearly that would be absurd. Yet Arnold was in fact a very typical nineteenth-century English intellectual – more earnest and more talented than most – but sufficiently representative to be of general and not merely particular interest. How is one to sum up the relationship of the author of *Dover Beach* to his society?

Try jotting down a sentence or two.
(a)   Does the imagination of this poet operate within the conventions of the ruling class in the way Wyatt's does?
(b)   Do we have here another example, like Blake, of the artist as revolutionary?
(c)   Would you describe *Dover Beach* as the work of a 'committed' artist?
(d)   Or does Matthew Arnold turn away from the society he lives in?

I think the interesting thing about this poem (from the point of view we are concerned with) is that while public and private experiences are to a considerable extent fused, it is ultimately to the private *as opposed to* the public life that the poet turns. He begins by calling out his wife to share with him the emotions which are evoked by Dover Beach: they are part of the situation and its history – just as Wyatt and his lover are part of the sixteenth-century court-situation and Blake a part of the London of 1793. But by the end of the poem Arnold has made a decisive turn away from the social world. Wyatt, by implication, resents the social world within which he lives; Blake, more explicitly, loathes and condemns commercial London. But neither poses the possibility of some alternative sphere of reality, somewhere 'safe', immune from the pressures and problems of society as a whole. Matthew Arnold, on the other hand, can neither reconcile himself to his society nor see the possibility of changing it. The 'resolution' of his poem involves a sort of sidestep into a quite different realm:

> Ah, love, let us be true
> To one another!

A private world of fidelity and trust is sought because the public world is so unpleasant, hostile, unpromising.

Now one may argue, of course, that there is nothing specifically Victorian about this situation: withdrawal to a private world to avoid the difficulties of society at large. Isn't it, for instance, what Romeo and Juliet, and star-crossed lovers through the ages, try to do? I think there is a difference. Romeo and Juliet, it is true, find themselves upon a darkling plain, swept with confused alarms of struggle and flight where the armies of Montagues and Capulets clash, both by day and night. But Shakespeare, their creator, does not imply for a moment that Romeo and Juliet can succeed in finding a world of personal bliss immune from social pressures. On the contrary, the whole burden of his play is that either the feuds of the great families must be resolved or else boys and girls like Romeo and Juliet can never be happy, and the play ends in fact with the promise (however dim) of a new society presided over by the impartial Duke. In other words, Shakespeare does not suggest for a moment that private life and public life can be separated.

Figure 9
Matthew Arnold by
G. F. Watts (National
Portrait Gallery)

Arnold's position is more ambiguous. On the one hand he is very much aware of the social world (and in his own public life worked conscientiously as an educational reformer): on the other he seems to feel a sort of superiority towards it. Those armies sweeping the plains are, above all, 'ignorant' and the word is used, as it still often is today, to suggest not only a lack of knowledge of the facts but a sort of general inferiority. ('O, he's an ignorant devil' implies not only that he doesn't know what he needs to know but that it's not much use trying to teach him.) This particular use of the word ignorant is interesting, for in it two meanings are involved. On the one hand 'ignorant' means simply 'not knowing' and as such is a relatively neutral concept, not necessarily involving any moral or social judgement. On the other 'ignorant' in certain contexts takes on a number of social implications, involving a sense of the speaker's disapproval. (The word 'uneducated' has similar problems. It *may* be used quite neutrally to describe the state of having little or no education. But once being uneducated comes to have a sort of *social* significance, involving an ignorance of what the speaker thinks *ought* to be known by a socially respectable person, then to call a person 'uneducated' is not to make a morally neutral statement.) In Matthew Arnold's use of the word here there is (or don't you agree?) a suggestion that these armies he is talking about are not merely ignorant in the sense of lacking knowledge but that their ignorance takes forms which the poet finds socially menacing. It is the sense of something menacing the values of the world he feels at home in which leads this individual to wish to withdraw from the public social world to a private one where the fidelity of lovers is enough.

The position of the artist in nineteenth-century Europe (as you will gather from the discussion of 'Arts and Society in an Age of Industrialization' in the later part of this Course) was a curious one. There has probably never been a period in which the artists thrown up by a society were more continuously critical of that society. Almost all the great figures of Victorian literature and painting felt to some degree hostile to Victorian society: some – like Dickens and Ruskin and William Morris – expressed their criticisms openly; another response was to try to create, as in Tennyson's poem, a 'palace of art' where the beauty which could not be found in actual life could be created and preserved. In this situation the artist tended to be thought of – both by the general public and himself – as a kind of licensed oddity. In his personal life he was often a bohemian, living and even dressing in ways frowned upon by 'respectable' society: and he himself tended to despise society and to see his freedom in terms of independence from normal social obligations. Hence the curious flavour – still remaining today – of the word 'artistic' when used by non-artists about those who practise art.

Basic to these tendencies in the development of the artist's role seems to be the increasing separation between public and private life. Before the nineteenth century the artist, by and large, had an accepted role within the framework of aristocratic society. Chaucer, Shakespeare, Milton, Pope all lived and worked as social beings with a more or less clearly defined place within the social world of their day and not far from the centres of power. This is not to say that they were uncritical of what was going on around them or might not indeed (like Milton) be committed to revolutionary social change. But the ideas of *rejection* of social ties or of art as operating in a sphere of its own are foreign to them. The societies in which they operate are complex and their attitudes are complex too. They may feel compelled to take sides in the social conflicts of their time. But they do not in a fundamental way see the individual and society as opposing forces. The nineteenth-century artist was not so sure.

STUDY NOTE 5: QUOTING (by Ellie Mace)

Arnold Kettle has now given two further instances of the artist's relationship to his society (Blake and Arnold, in addition to Wyatt earlier on). Each time his first concern is that you understand the meaning of the poems, because until you do there is no point in his going any further. (The same applies to work you might do on an historical document, a piece of music or a painting.) Thereafter he develops his theme (stated on p. 33 and noted in Study Note 4) by asking the kind of questions that focus your attention on the relationship of the artist to his society (for example, the set of four questions on p. 48), and by drawing comparisons and contrasts between them (for instance, the discussion of Blake and Wyatt on pp. 44–45). You'll notice that he often uses the words of the poets to illustrate the points he is making about their poems and their 'positions'. This is not to be confused with plagiarism. Arnold Kettle makes it quite clear that he is using the poet's words by placing quotation marks round them or by indenting them, as on p. 48.

> Ah, love, let us be true
> To one another!

Indenting is normally used when more than one line of poetry (or a passage of prose) is being quoted. Notice that quotation marks are not necessary if the lines are indented. If you want to quote only a word or two then you incorporate the quotation into your own sentence using quotation marks – for example on p. 47: 'The evocation of calm in the opening lines (the important words "calm", "fair", "tranquil", "sweet") gradually broken or modified (with the word "only") by the "eternal note of sadness" . . .' etc. Here Arnold Kettle is quoting these words from the poem in order to give force to the point he wants to make about it – he has a feeling of calm and he is trying to show what gave him this feeling – to explain and provide 'evidence' or support for this belief about the poem. You'll notice that he rarely uses quotations of more than a few lines and commonly quotes only a word or two at a time. He is *using* quotation to back up or illustrate *his* thoughts about the poem – not to show that he's learnt great chunks of it, or because he can't find words of his own.

Sometimes in an essay you may want to quote from a unit author, or a sentence or two from a set book. This is fine provided there is good reason to do so and you don't do too much of it. If the author neatly sums up a point you wish to make yourself, or on the other hand you want to disagree with something he/she has said, you may need to quote the actual words. But if your tutor thinks you are using the author's words too often, or without apparent reason, then even though you are quoting and not plagiarizing you may well be penalized. There will not be enough indication in your essay that *you* have thoughts and ideas about the question.

Finally, there may be passages in what you have just read that you feel you do not understand, or are worried about in some way, even though you have read them carefully more than once. Whenever this happens you should not hesitate to ask for help from your tutor-counsellor and fellow students.

THE ARTIST AND SOCIETY (by Arnold Kettle) CONTINUED

The Artist as Exile

Our final example is taken, quite significantly, from a book about an artist, James Joyce's *Portrait of the Artist as a Young Man* (1916). I used the word 'significantly' because the sort of self-consciousness about 'the position of the artist' inherent in the whole conception of Joyce's book is in itself a part of the phenomenon we are considering. Books about artists and their dilemmas have become a feature of European cultural life of the last hundred years.

Joyce's novel recounts the development of a young Irishman, Stephen Dedalus, who, after a Roman Catholic education, decides that his true vocation is that of an artist. The book is obviously to a considerable extent autobiographical, but although Stephen's views on art may well represent those of James Joyce at a stage in his development, we should not assume that they can be taken to express Joyce's own mature views on art. It is with Stephen, then, as Joyce creates him, rather than with Joyce himself that we are concerned.

The discussion on art from which the two short passages we shall be looking at are taken comes in the final chapter of the book which is about Stephen's decision to reject most of the values of the life around him and to devote himself to art. He is by now a student at University College, Dublin, and his decisions are thrashed out during a series of conversations with his friends, also students, especially Lynch and Cranly. These conversations have great emotional force within the context of the novel, for what is involved is not an abstract argument but a battle between conflicting ways of living. In removing the passages from their context we will inevitably miss much of this compelling force: but the issues Stephen raises and the view of the artist he expresses remain just as significant, even abstracted from the total effect of the novel.

First, then, a sentence in which Stephen sums up to his friend Lynch his view of aesthetics:

> The artist, like the God of the creation, remains within or behind or beyond or above his handwork, invisible, refined out of existence, indifferent, paring his fingernails.

The artist as God, and an indifferent God at that: is the essence of the sentence. And it is followed, some pages later, by Stephen's conversation with another friend, Cranly:

> . . . Look here, Cranly, he said. You have asked me what I would do and what I would not do. I will tell you what I will do and what I will not do. I will not serve that in which I no longer believe, whether it call itself my home, my fatherland, or my church: and I will try to express myself in some mode of life or art as freely as I can and as wholly as I can, using for my defence the only arms I allow myself to use – silence, exile and cunning.

EXERCISE

When you have read these passages several times make notes which indicate what seem to you the chief features of the view of the artist expressed here. Then try the following questions:

1   What does Stephen mean when he says the artist, like a God, is 'indifferent'?
2   Express in your own words what to be an artist seems to mean to Stephen.

DISCUSSION

1   To answer this question properly one should, obviously, have read Joyce's *Portrait of the Artist;* but even without doing so one can legitimately examine the particular idea expressed here. The main points, I think, are (a) the notion that the work of art, once created, is autonomous, with a life and existence of its own and (b) the notion that the artist, the creator, like God, cannot by definition serve anything beyond himself.

The artist is indifferent in the sense that his art is self-justifying: it does not exist (to use Auden's thought) to make something happen. The artist is not 'committed', presumably beforehand, to some course of action or belief which his art must serve. He is indifferent to the consequences of his art because, like God, he is responsible to nobody but himself. You cannot say God *ought* to do something because only God (by definition) can know what he ought to do: and it is the same with the artist in the sense that he is a creator. And having created his work of art he can do nothing about it except, presumably, recreate or destroy it.

2   Stephen, as in the preceding passage, is making the highest possible claim not only for the artist (who is like God) but for the individual who alone can decide what he will reject and what he will believe in. Stephen here is rejecting the three major sources of authority in the modern world: church, state and family. Like Lucifer rejecting the power of the Almighty, Stephen refuses to serve. And parallel to this rejection of service or commitment comes the vow of

self-expression – free and complete – and the interesting choice of 'weapons' – silence, exile and cunning – all of which emphasize the lone quality of the artist's life and his suspicion of and rejection by the majority.

Figure 10   James Joyce (right) as a student at University College Dublin, with two of his friends (Croessman Collection of James Joyce, Southern Illinois University)

It is tempting, on the basis of these passages, to say that Stephen is rejecting all forms of social obligation and indeed denying that the artist is a social being at all. But if you have read the passages carefully you will have realized that such a description would not be quite true. Stephen does not say that he will serve nothing: he says he will not serve 'that in which I no longer believe'. And Joyce's *Portrait* is in fact very firmly set in a definite place and time so that the reader of the book knows very well that what Stephen has particularly in mind is his own family, Irish nationalism and the Roman Catholic Church. So he is, at least theoretically, leaving himself a loophole: he would serve something he could believe in, though in fact the only thing he can find to believe in is art.

Again, the words 'silence, exile and cunning' are words which have a social context, even though a negative one. To keep silent is one form of contribution to an argument: it implies an attitude. Exile implies a certain relationship to a place from which one is exiled. Cunning suggests some form of rebellion, or at least of tactics. So that the life Stephen sees ahead is not one of total isolation from society as such. Rather it is a life of conscious non-conformity and scepticism about the established order. And there is no suggestion that in the battle he is to fight (for 'arms' imply a battle) he will find solidarity with any other human beings. In this he is unlike the protagonist in *Dover Beach* who turns to his lover for what the public world cannot provide or Blake who, in his powerful feelings of indignation, aligns himself with the chimney sweeper, the soldier and the new-born infant. Stephen's position might be described as one of *almost* total withdrawal from social obligation and of emphasis on the validity of the individual *as opposed to* the social criteria of judgement.

As far as the situation of the artist goes, Stephen Dedalus's position might be said to be so far as possible from that of the creators of art in primitive societies. *They* could not conceive of man except as a social being or of art except as having a communal function. *He* admits, though grudgingly, that man is a social being but is far more conscious of what separates him from other men than of what binds him to them. To the primitive artist freedom means service to the tribe for he does not think of himself except as a member of the tribe: to Stephen freedom means freeing himself *from* the society he was born into. Many twentieth-century artists seek freedom through the achievement of their own 'identity' rather than through some form of commitment to a social purpose.

I do not want to draw many *general* conclusions from the material we have been examining. For one thing, we have been looking at only a few examples and a much wider knowledge of the subject is necessary before one is in a position to test general statements. For another, the object of this exercise is to invite you to think about the questions raised rather than to offer you cut-and-dried formulae. Nevertheless, we should try to draw together some of the ideas we have been considering.

You will have noticed that, although the different examples we have examined indicate different relationships between the artist and his society, all of them involve *some* relationship. Even when the final appeal is to the integrity of a personal emotion, as in *Dover Beach* or *A Portrait of the Artist*, the protagonist remains, however unwillingly, a social being taking up a stance which implicitly accepts this fact. And indeed it seems impossible to deny that we are all of us social beings, standing in some sort of relation to other human beings. Man cannot exist in isolation: if he tried to the species would die out. So the question we are faced with is not 'Does the artist have a relationship to society?' but 'What kind of relationship does he have?'

EXERCISE

Do you think one can sum up the answer to the question at the end of the preceding sentence in a single pronouncement which defines satisfactorily the role of the artist in society? Yes or No? If so, give your definition: if not, say why you can't.

DISCUSSION

(a)   If you have said 'Yes' then I think you will find that the only sort of definition you can produce is one that is so general that it is not really a definition at all.

(b)   You might, for instance, make a very general statement of the sort Shelley produced when he said that 'poets are the unacknowledged legislators of the world'. This is a noble sentiment and may well be true but it doesn't take us very far towards an analytical definition. Or you may have come up with some such phrase as 'artists act as the conscience of society'. This, again, is very vague. It doesn't tell us in what sense the artist acts as a society's conscience. And it is most doubtful whether many societies or many artists have ever regarded the relationship in this light.

(c)   There are two very strong reasons why the answer 'No' is, at the very least, the safer one. One is that the function of the artist and his own views of his role have changed so much in the course of human history. The second is that there are – and apparently have always been – so many different sorts of art that it is not satisfactory to lump them all together. The role of the artist who designed the Parthenon and that of Charlie Chaplin in his films are too far apart to be covered by any but the most general definition. Even if one says that the architect of the Parthenon and Charlie Chaplin both served society in their different ways, one hasn't really said very much.

This does not mean, however, that it is impossible to say anything valid or interesting about the relationship of art to social life as a whole. It is important, for instance, to recognise that it is a *changing* relationship, and our examples, if looked at together, seem to indicate that whereas in relatively simple societies in which, for instance, physical and mental activity are still very closely associated, art is seen as part of the practice of the tribe, in later societies the artist is likely to be faced with a more complex situation. This is true, we should remember, not only of the artist but of people in general. The situation – sometimes summed up by the word 'alienation' – in which the individual feels himself to be divided from the social processes, rather than seeing them as essential to his self-fulfilment, is not peculiar to the artist, though – just because he *is* an artist – he may be more aware of it and articulate this sense more clearly than other people. It is certainly a significant fact that many artists in the last hundred years in Europe and North America have felt it to be quite natural that the artist should be at odds with his society and that some have carried this attitude to the length of holding that the true artist is bound to be at odds with society as such – *any* society. But whether this fact tells us more about 'the artist and society' in general or about a particular phase of human development is the kind of problem you will have to think out for yourself.

STUDY NOTE 6: NOTE TAKING (by Ellie Mace)

I've already pointed out that your answers to questions in the text can sometimes be used in essays and that they are a form of note taking – written records of your ideas to which you can return. But there will be sections of units in which no exercises are set and these may contain points or arguments that you think are crucial and wish to record (this applies particularly to parts of the subject matter you have to write essays about, or will be examined on). If you are making notes with, for example, a particular TMA question in mind, then you will record what is relevant to that question and ignore the rest. But let's suppose that you want to make notes on a section of the text in order just to have a record of the main points and ideas to use as a reminder, or because you found it complicated and want to have it clear in your mind.

The essence of note taking is to record the *main* points, with one or two bits of supporting material, and to make clear the connections between those points, or the main direction of the arguments. There is very little point in making a set of notes that are as long (or even longer!) than the text itself. You might just as well reread the text. With this in mind I suggest you try making a set of notes for *The Artist as Exile* (pp. 51–54). (Do not include your answers to the questions on p. 52 because you'll have these written down anyway). My own attempt follows.

Notes on pp. 51–54 Unit 1, A101, *The Artist as Exile* – based on James Joyce *Portrait of the Artist as a Young Man* (1916) last chapter: conversation re 'the position of the artist' or 'ways of living'

1   Artist as (indifferent) God

'The artist, like the God of creation, . . . paring his fingernails.'

    i.e. – wk. of art is autonomous – has life of own

       – creator (artist) serves only his art

       (N.B. s.p.n.* on theme – no social commitment)

2   parallel position of individual

'I will not serve that in which I no longer believe . . . silence, exile, and cunning.'

    i.e. – individ. decide what he believes in: reject auth. of church, state, family; be self, express self

    ∴ he is a non-conformist and to that extent cut off fr. others
    (tho' not *totally* isolated – recognizes society (∵ setting self against it)
              – will serve his art)

Concl.	primitive artists	20th c. artists
FREEDOM	service to the tribe	freedom *from* soc.
	(s.p.n. – reference)	(any other examples)

*Key: s.p.n. = see previous notes (plus reference)

    . . . (in quotation) indicates some words have been left out

    re = about   wk. = work   ∴ = therefore   ∵ = because
    i.e. = that is   N.B. = take note

If I'd been making these notes for myself I'd have abbreviated many more words and included some remarks of my own (for example in the 'boxes' under Conclusion) – e.g. what about artists who are not 'alienated' in this way?

Your version may *look* quite different from mine – some people prefer to make notes that look like diagrams (or more like my concluding 'boxes'). But I don't think your version should be much longer or more detailed than mine, if it's to be useful as a set of *notes*. Had the section of text been longer I would have included page or margin numbers against each main point in my notes so that I could easily refer back to the text if I needed to add, or check, points of detail.

As with most of these 'study techniques' your job is to work out the best way for *you* to proceed. Start experimenting now if you're not used to making notes and, again, don't be afraid to ask for advice from your tutor-counsellor and fellow students at the Study Centre.

CONCLUSION (by Arthur Marwick)

Finally, let me stress that 'The Artist and Society' has simply been presented here as an example of the sort of issue (though a very central one) that students of the humanities are expected to be involved with, and, above all, to show the way in which it is necessary to bring in several disciplines in order to deal with this topic adequately. The main disciplines involved, obviously, were literature and history; but Arnold Kettle also skilfully strengthened his discussion by references to architecture and to other arts.

Most of this unit has been about basic approaches to the study of the arts. The first assignment, which you should embark on now, is designed to get you to put some of these approaches into practice and also to make use of some of the ideas about the relationship between the artist and the society and age in which he lived raised by Arnold Kettle. You then proceed to Unit 2B which is primarily concerned with that part of our second aim which referred to the importance of 'clear and logical thinking'.

A101 AN ARTS FOUNDATION COURSE

ARTS AND SOCIETY IN AN AGE OF INDUSTRIALIZATION